I0714421

ILLUSTRATION by
W.H. CHONG

This project was assisted by the University of Technology Sydney Library, through an artist residency grant awarded to Zoë Sadokierski in 2015.

First published in 2015 *by*
BOOKWORK PRESS
WEB: **www.bookworkpress.com**
EMAIL: zoe.sadokierski@gmail.com

with the support of
SYDNEY WRITERS' FESTIVAL
WEB: **www.swf.org.au**

National Library of Australia
Cataloguing-in-Publication entry
The book of days : an illustrated anthology from
the 2015 Sydney Writers' Festival / editor Zoë Sadokierski.
ISBN: 9780994286758 (PB)
Sydney Writers Festival.
Art festivals--New South Wales--Sydney.
Authors, Australian.
Creative writing.
Anthologies.
A820.8

COVER AND INTERNAL DESIGN: Zoë Sadokierski
Essay text set in Fairfield 11/16pt.
Margin text set in National

THE BOOK OF DAYS

AN ILLUSTRATED ANTHOLOGY FROM THE 2015 SYDNEY WRITERS' FESTIVAL

EDITED by
ZOË SADOKIERSKI

ILLUSTRATIONS:

CONTENTS

How to Live?

JEMMA BIRRELL

—

FOREWORD *from*
SYDNEY WRITERS' FESTIVAL
ARTISTIC DIRECTOR

—

OVER THE PAST few years I've been thinking about why literary festivals are so important. At the heart of the festival is our love of books. Reading is a solitary pursuit, but at the same time, in a sort of blissful contradiction, festivals bring all of us together in one time and place, as a community. Sydney Writers' Festival is one of those rare places today where there's a genuine exchange between readers and writers. It's an utterly freewheeling mix of ideas and I don't think we get that in many other places.

The theme of the 2015 Sydney Writers' Festival was **How to Live?** Where do we find a sense of purpose and how should we best live our lives? More than 400 writers helped us make sense of the world, exploring ideas of happiness, grief, spirituality, our relationship with nature, technology and our own mortality.

We welcomed writers from Australia and all over the globe—from Nigeria, Norway, Canada, the UK, Indonesia, the Middle East, America and Europe. We heard from a novelist who bends genres and time itself, from poets whose words transport, a mortician who helped us face the reality of death, a foreign correspondent who spent the past 28 years reporting in the Middle East, from the winner of the Man Booker Prize and from writers who bring so much joy to children.

One of the wonderful things about the festival is also the chance to discover writers you don't know you're missing yet and uncover new ideas and perspectives, so I hope you get a taste of that in *The Book of Days*.

THE
BOOK
OF DAYS

THE
BOOK
OF DAYS

THE
BOOK
OF DAYS

THE
BOOK
OF DAYS

when you can't
enter through
the front door,
Kick in a
window.
LIZ
FICHERA

WRITING
STATION
How to Live?

THE BOOK OF DAYS
WWW.BOOKWORKPRESS.COM

THE BOOK OF DAYS
SWF
BOD
CONTRIBUTE BY RESPONDING
TO THE THEME HOW TO LIVE?
VIA TWITTER #SWFBOD OR
AT THIS WRITING STATION
WWW.BOOKWORKPRESS.COM

THE
BOOK
OF DAYS

THE BOOK OF DAYS

Introduction

ZOË SADOKIERSKI

—

This anthology celebrates writers, readers and the spontaneous community that forms when we come together.

—

PHOTOGRAPHS *by*
JACKSON MANN

THE BOOK OF DAYS is an illustrated anthology from the 2015 Sydney Writers' Festival. The book was designed live during the festival at a workstation next to the Pier 2/3 Main Stage at Walsh Bay.

The anthology is divided into two parts. The first is a selection of writing and illustrations from festival presenters. It includes excerpts of what was read or shown at festival events, previously published poems or essays, and a few tastes of as-yet unpublished work.

The second part is a selection of writing and images from festival audiences in response to the theme, How to Live? These contributions were submitted via Twitter (using #SWFBOD) or on typewriters and index cards at the writing station.

As a whole, the book is a memento of the festival experience, a record of what was presented and also how it was received. Writers and readers, together.

THE CONCEPT

CHRISTIANITY, JUDAISM and ISLAM are all religions of the book: at the heart of each is a holy book that instructs followers on how to live. I don't follow an organised religion, but the 2015 Sydney Writers' Festival theme made me realise that I belong to a religion of the book as well. More accurately, a religion of books. I find ideas about how to live through reading: novels, biographies, essays, newspapers, magazines and even social media.

I borrowed the idea for *The Book of Days* from a Christian devotional text known as a Book of Hours, a collection of psalms, hymns, prayers and readings that offer guidance on how to live a moral life. The hours refer to eight separate devotional passages intended to be recited at the eight canonical hours of the day: the wee hours, dawn, mid-morning, late morning, noon, mid-afternoon, sundown, late evening. In medieval times a Book of Hours was the only book that most lay families could afford to own, and most people learned to read from one.

Each passage of text is framed by a border of intricate illustrations depicting key themes or events. These are known as illuminations. More than illustrations of the written text, the illuminations transform each spread into a surface for meditation and reflection.

THE CREATIVE PROCESS

THE BOOK YOU HOLD in your hands was created from scratch in three weeks. In the days before the festival, I collected contributions from festival presenters, commissioned illustrators and set up the workstation down at Walsh Bay. Once the festival was underway, I designed these pages with a monitor attached to the computer so audiences could watch the book taking shape in real time. At the same time I gathered responses from passers-by either on Twitter, index cards or on one of the two typewriters on the table in front of me. Monica Monin and Astrid Lorange kept me company while working on the Living Index (*see pages 136–143*), Leigh Rigozzi put in hours both at the desk and in festival sessions creating his wonderful illustrations, and a rotating cast of illustrators stopped by to contribute.

The production continued when the festival came to an end: typing up audience contributions (about 4000 words all up); scanning and laying out illustrations (all those dinosaurs took half a day alone); editing the text; making additional illustrations and creating print-ready files.

As well as a souvenir of the 2015 festival, this anthology is a compelling argument for the future of books in print. By the time the next Sydney Writers' Festival comes around, there will be a new program on the website, the previous year's newspaper lift-outs will be yellowed and all the news and conversations about the 2015 experience will be buried deep in the ether. This anthology, though, will remain on my shelf, and hopefully yours too. I will remember the authors I heard, the people I met and the experience of being swept up in a community of readers. This book will be on my shelf for years to come because book objects are talismans as much as vessels for the content they carry. What better way to celebrate a writers' festival than in book form?

A book like this is a collaborative effort. I want to thank those who supported the project and me, since all of this was done on a wing and a prayer. From the start, Jemma Birrell and Kate Steinweg were enthusiastic and instrumental in organising author contributions, along with other festival staff including Tim Barker, Andy Lysle and Rani Haywood. Ashleigh Wilson provided editorial and general support.

I've published this book myself using the print-on-demand service Blurb.com. This means when someone wants a book, they order it online via the Blurb website, it gets printed and shipped to them. There is no 'print run'; the book only exists when someone orders one. Any profits generated from book sales will be donated to the Sydney Writers' Festival, a charity organisation, to support future events and projects.

Other than *'where are the toilets?'* the question I was asked most during the Festival was *'what's with the dancing donkeys / rabbits / monkeys?* The Zodiac sign for late-May is Gemini. The Twins. At Sydney Writers' Festival, held May 18–24, two sets of pairings come to mind that are relevant for an illlustrated anthology: writers and readers; words and images. Festivals are celebrations, hence the dancing.

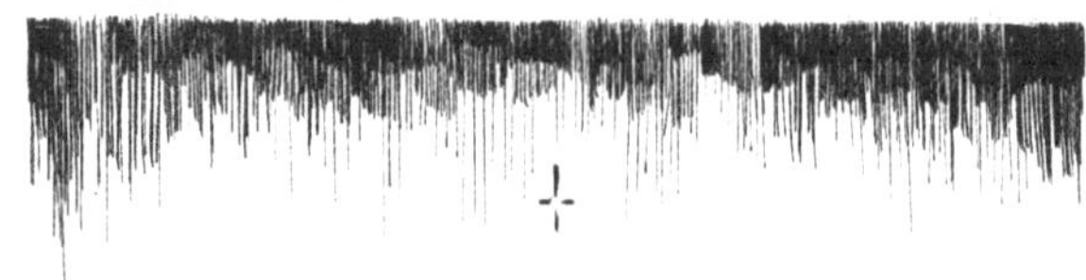

EX LIBRIS:

YAN QIN WENG

'DESERT' *from the Ex Libris series*

EX LIBRIS (2012) *is a series of illustrations examining the idea of books as indicators of human presence, signals in a familiar language soon to be (we speculate) endangered. They are drawn in the style of traditional bookplates to evoke connections with ownership and belonging, but the books within are abandoned in locations incongruous to their nature. The term 'Ex Libris' means 'from the library of ...'— but where are these books from? To whom do they belong?*

WWW.3DAYSMARCH.NET

PART ONE

SELECTED WRITING *from* FESTIVAL PRESENTERS

2015 OPENING ADDRESS
MOHSIN HAMID: LIFE IN THE TIME OF PERMAWAR
6:30 – 7:30 PM TUES, MAY 19
ROSLYN PACKER THEATRE
HICKSON RD, WALSH BAY

Also appeared at:
— *MOHSIN HAMID: LIFE, POLITICS, ART AND FICTION*
— *EXTREMISM: WHAT ARE WE DEALING WITH?*

MOHSIN HAMID has written three novels, *Moth Smoke*, *The Reluctant Fundamentalist* which was shortlisted for the Man Booker Prize, and *How to Get Filthy Rich in Rising Asia*, as well as a book of essays, *Discontent and Its Civilizations*. He has been a winner or finalist of more than 20 awards, and his books have been featured on bestseller lists, adapted for the cinema, and translated into 35 languages. Born in Lahore, he has also lived in London, New York, and California.

AN EXCERPT FROM THE OPENING ADDRESS:

Life in the Time of Permawar

MOHSIN HAMID

Humanity's traditional sources of solace are being disrupted. How then, are we to live?

SO YOU ARE A READER, A WRITER, in this, the time of the Permawar, searching among other things for empathy, for transcendence, for encounters that need not divide us into clans, for stories that can be told around a campfire generous enough for seven billion, stories that transcend divisions, question the self and the boundaries of groups, stories that are a shared endeavor not at the level of the tribe but of the human, that remind us we are not adversaries, we are in it together, the great mass murderer, Death, has us all in its sights, and we would do well not to allow ourselves willingly to be its instruments, but instead to recognize one another with compassion, not as predatory cannibals but as meals for the same shark, each with a limited, precious time to abide, a time that deserves our respect and our wonder, a time that is a story, each of us a story, each of them a story, and each of these other stories, quite possibly, just as unique, just as frightened, as tiny, as vast as our own.

Dynamic Rest

LES MURRAY

ILLUSTRATION *by*
W.H. CHONG

Originally published in
Waiting for the Past, 2015

LES MURRAY is the author of *Waiting for the Past*, his first new volume of poems since 2010's *Taller When Prone*. He has published some thirty books. His work is studied in schools and universities around Australia and has been translated into several foreign languages. In 1996 he was awarded the T.S. Eliot Prize for poetry, in 1998 the Queen's Gold Medal for poetry, and in 2004 the Mondello Prize. He lives in Bunyah, near Taree in New South Wales.

Appeared at:
— *THE WORLD IN THREE POETS*
— *LES MURRAY: WAITING FOR THE PAST*

ILLUSTRATION *by*
ZOË SADOKIERSKI

Dynamic Rest

Six little terns
feet gripping sand
on a windy beach

six more just above
white with opened wings
busy exchange of feet

reaching down lifting off
terns rising up through terns
all quivering parallel

drift ahead and settle
bracing their eyes
against the brunt of wind

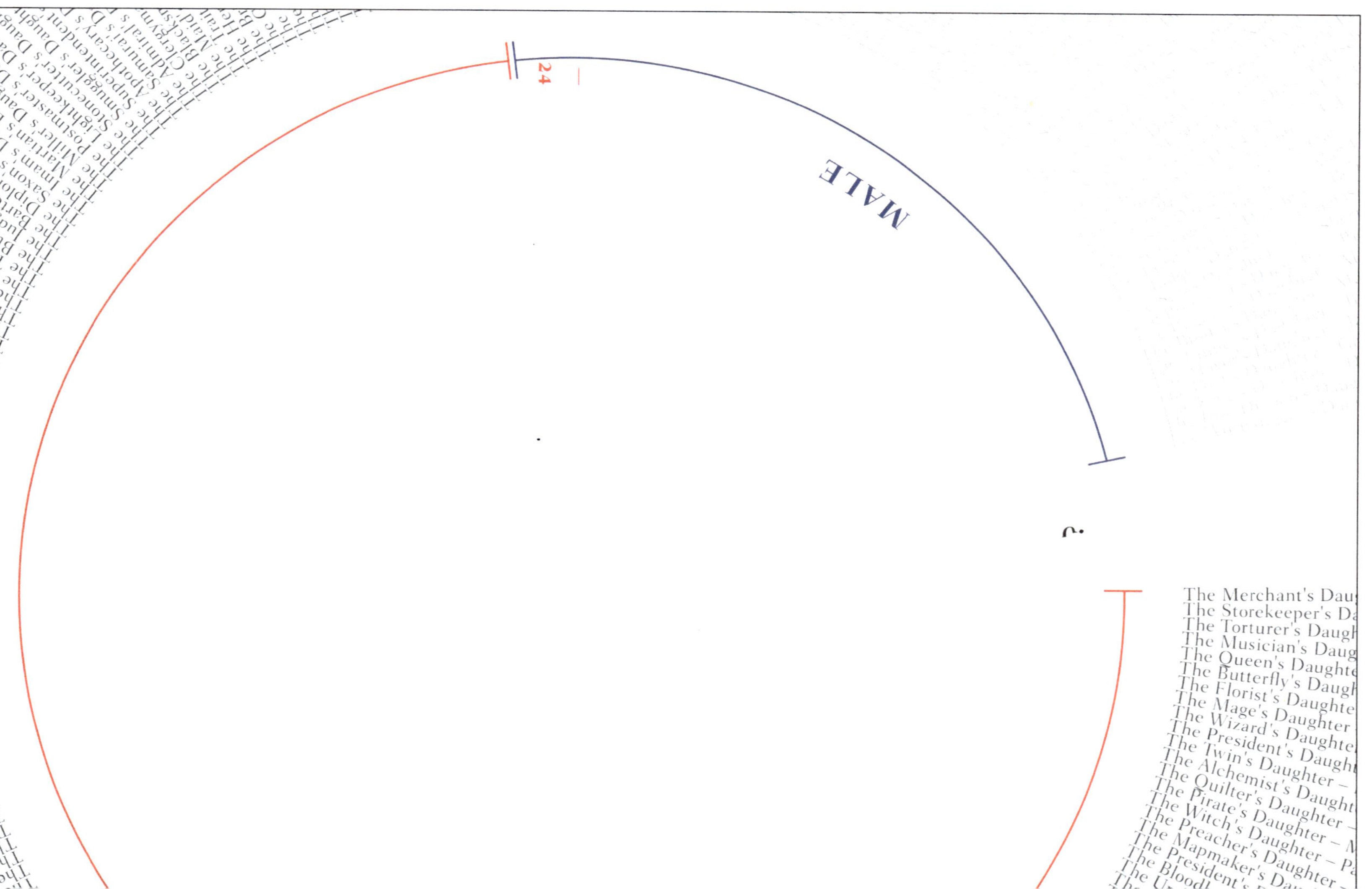
MALE

The ______'s Daughter

EMILY ST. JOHN MANDEL

—

Originally published in *The Millions*
www.themillions.com

—

Appeared at:
— *SWF NIGHT OF LISTENING: STORYTELLING WITH SOUND*
— *IMAGINED FUTURES*
— *ON PANDEMICS*
— *EMILY ST. JOHN MANDEL: ART AND SURVIVAL*

EMILY ST. JOHN MANDEL was born and raised on the west coast of British Columbia, Canada. Her fourth novel, ***Station Eleven***, was a 2014 National Book Award Finalist and *The Singer's Gun* won the 2014 Prix Mystere de la Critique in France. Her short fiction and essays have been anthologised in numerous collections, including *Best American Mystery Stories* 2013. She is a staff writer for *The Millions* and lives in New York City with her husband.

1.

TITLES HAVE A WAY of coming in waves. There was a time a few years back when it seemed like vast numbers of books were being published on the subject of secret lives, as in *The Secret Life of Bees*, *The Secret Lives of Buildings*, *The Secret Lives of Words*, etc. Our literature seems to hold a parallel obsession with vanishing, which involves of course any number of titles involving the words 'Disappear' or 'Vanishing' or 'Lost.'

But no trend has seemed quite so pervasive as the daughter phenomenon. Seriously, once you start noticing them, they're everywhere. I'm Facebook friends with the authors of *The Hummingbird's Daughter*, *The Baker's Daughter*, *The Calligrapher's Daughter*, and *The Murderer's Daughters*, and those are just the ones I can think of off the top of my head.

I was curious to see how many of these books there actually are, so I did a search for books with 'The' and 'Daughter' in their titles on Goodreads, a popular American website for readers with an extensive database of books.

Afterward I spent some time copying and pasting all instances of The ___'s Daughter into an Excel spreadsheet. How much time? A lot, because I'm studying a foreign language, and cutting and pasting text is exactly the kind of mindless activity that can be done while I'm listening to language podcasts.

I was careful to collect only books that adhered to the 'The ___'s Daughter' formula. So I didn't include *The Murderer's*

Daughters, for example, or *The Kitchen Daughter*. Even leaving those variations out, though, the number of The ___'s Daughter books out there is truly staggering. By the time I stopped—and I was only on page 88 of 200 pages of search results—I was left with 530 titles.

2.

TO BE CLEAR, I think there's absolutely nothing wrong with calling one's book The ___'s Daughter. I think those titles have a marvelous rhythm to them. And yet I couldn't help but wonder why there seemed to be so many of them.

Where to begin? I could ask any of the four or five authors I know with Daughter titles, but as a general rule I hesitate to ask any author to comment publicly on either the title or the cover art of their books—these are things that authors don't necessarily have much control over. If it should happen that an author doesn't love the title they end up with, this isn't something they can really talk about publicly without alienating their publisher.

No authors, then, because I don't want to put anyone in an awkward position. I turned, as I like to do whenever a publishing-related question arises, to the booksellers. Partly because I know a lot of independent booksellers and they're some of my favourite people, and partly I've noticed they're much more outspoken about publishing than most people in the publishing business are. It's a refreshing quality.

I spoke with the manager of WORD, a popular bookstore in New York City. I was curious as to whether The ____'s Daughter books sell better than other titles, or if there was any other advantage she could think of. Her theory, she told me, is that familiar-sounding titles drive sales, because they help give readers a small feeling of comfort when they're contemplating which book to purchase out of the thousands and thousands available. She suggested that perhaps repeated words, like 'daughter,' give an overwhelmed person standing in front of a new fiction table a place to start. And it goes double for the books with the empty shoes and the headless girls in sundresses on the cover, she said. If you've had a good experience with one in the past, it makes sense to try some-thing similar on your next trip.

She's right, I realized, there are an awful lot of headless girls in sundresses on the covers of contemporary fiction, although I hadn't noticed the empty shoes. What I found fascinating was that she said she'd never had a customer mix up the daughters in these books' titles. Apparently no one comes into the store looking for *The Apothecary's Daughter* when they mean *The Apostate's Daughter.*

Perhaps, then, there's something about the rhythm and construction of these titles that aids memory, which means that naming your book The ___'s Daughter is a very sensible thing to do. Perhaps the construction is so familiar that the average reader, having seen dozens or even hundreds of these titles, only really has to remember one word; perhaps at a certain point the mind plugs in The and Daughter automatically.

3.

THERE IS A STEADY TRICKLE of these titles in every decade, from the early 1900s through to the present day, but my extremely unscientific and woefully incomplete data suggests that it's a growing trend. I sorted my list of 530 titles by date and fired up PowerPoint.

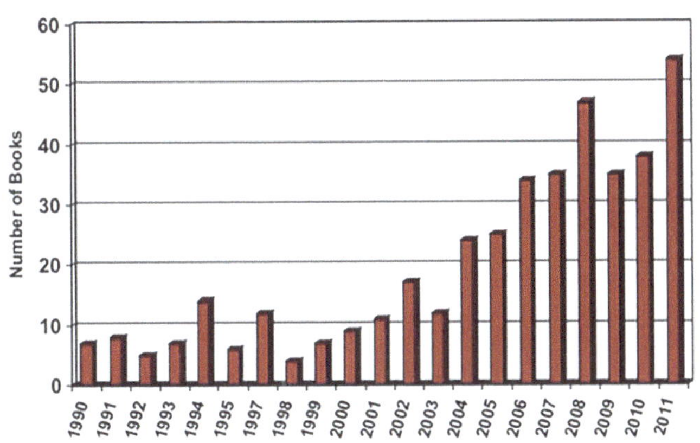

Fig. 1: Books Titled The ______'s Daughter, 1990-2011

One can of course go back much further, but previous decades are less dramatic and are also probably even less complete and even more wildly unscientific.

4.

I WAS CURIOUS to see if female authors were more likely to end up with a The __'s Daughter book than male authors, either because they chose the title themselves or because their editors chose the title for them. This called for a pie chart.

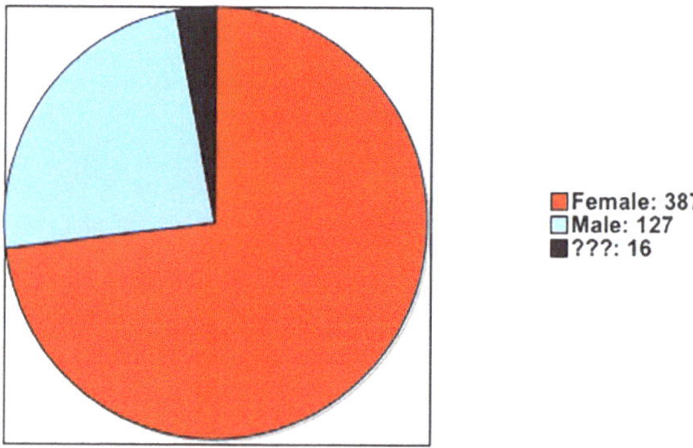

Fig. 2: Is the author of The ______'s Daughter a man or a woman?

Sometimes it's impossible to tell. There are authors who use initials instead of given names and maintain minimal web presences.

5.

WHAT I FOUND the most startling, aside from the sheer numbers, was the range of occupations, people, crimes, social classes, mythologies and attributes represented in these titles. I'm familiar with *The General's Daughter*, for instance, but *The Martian General's Daughter* was new to me. The identities of these daughters' parents ranged from the relatively mundane (*The Taxi Driver's Daughter*) to the wildly unexpected (*The Eiffel Tower's Daughter*).

When I looked over the list, certain patterns began to emerge. I started grouping titles into categories. Some categories — academics, servants, cartographers/explorers, and political activists, for instance—turned out to be quite small, just a handful of titles in each. On the other hand, the daughters of artists and artisans—lace-makers, musicians, painters, calligraphers—were particularly well-represented, as were the daughters of people connected to royalty (dukes, kings), and magical and/or supernatural entities (devils, centaurs, demons).

A great many parents represented on the list are politicians (e.g., *The Senator's Daughter, The Governor's Daughter*), or involved in the church (*The Bishop's Daughter, The Vicar's Daughter*). There are in fact several Vicar's Daughters. Prevailing trends in jacket art suggest that they're especially fond of low-cut blouses, but that's neither here nor there.

Then there's a large group of parents that's villainous and/ or on the wrong side of the law (*The Outlaw's Daughter, The*

Killer's Daughter), followed by a group employed as laborers (*The Miner's Daughter*), and a group that's affiliated with the military (*The Admiral's Daughter, The Colonel's Daughter*). A lot of them work with animals (*The Rancher's Daughter*), are possibly metaphorical (*The Sun's Daughter*), work in medicine (*The Emergency Doctor's Daughter*), or are employed in retail (*The Merchant's Daughter*).

The retailers are followed by three groups of exactly the same size: parents who do pseudo-sciencey things like astrology and alchemy (I'll let you guess these titles), parents in law enforcement or the judiciary (*The Sheriff's Daughter, The Judge's Daughter*), and parents who are keepers of either inns or lighthouses.

The last significant group involves parents who, to put the matter as delicately as possible, probably weren't married when their daughter was conceived (*The Harlot's Daughter, The Mistress's Daughter*).

But in case you skimmed these past few paragraphs, I have a graph for this too.

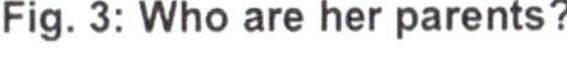
Fig. 3: Who are her parents?

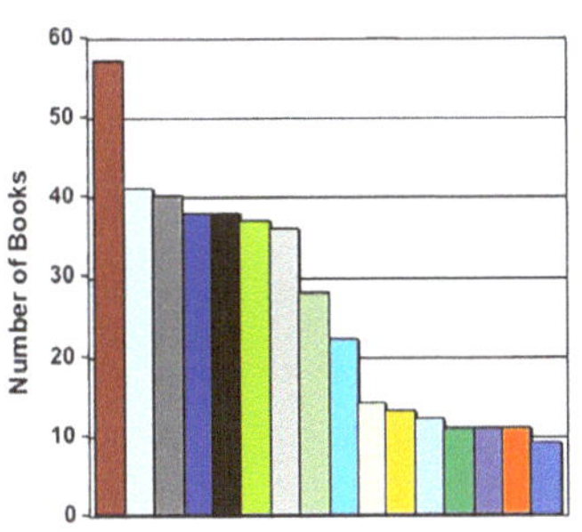
Number of Books
60
50
40
30
20
10
0
Artists or Artisans
Connected to royalty
Magical or supernatural
In politics
Involved with the church
Villainous and/or on the wrong side of the law
Laborers
Military
They work with animals
Possibly metaphorical
Medically inclined
They're in retail
They do pseudo-sciencey things like astrology and alchemy
In law enforcement or the judiciary
Keepers of either inns or lighthouses
Probably unmarried

Re-figuring The ______'s Daughter

GEMMA WARRINER

A visual interpretation of Emily St. John Mandel's research

GEMMA WARRINER is a Visual Communication Designer based in Sydney. Her work reflects her interests in information visualisation, food design and brand experience, where she seeks to engage, inform and delight an audience beyond the like-minded. Gemma graduated with an Honours degree in Visual Communication from the University of Technology Sydney in 2013 and has since been designing across both print and digital platforms.

comments sourced from
WWW.THEMILLIONS.COM

That's brilliant. You can never have too many graphs, even unscientific ones.
–Rhoda Baxter. 6:11am March 29 2012

Thanks for the charts and the work that went into them.
– Paulette. 10:27am March 30 2012

Dig the data analysis.
– Kerry. 12:58am April 3 2012

Oh, my word, I love this SO much. I have wondered the same thing! And I love graphs, so basically, this is heaven.
– RA. 9:45am April 5 2012

Have you considered sharing the Excel spreadsheet you created? I'd be very curious to see all of the many title variations!
– Julia at 12:55 pm on February 5 2014

I LOVE THAT EMILY shared her research visually with her readers. Looking at comments on *The Millions* it's clear others also appreciate this (see box on opposite page).

Emily sourced 530 titles adhering to the 'The ____'s Daughter' formula. Her infographics effectively visualise: 1. the growing trend of books titled 'The ____'s Daughter'; 2. the gender of the authors; and 3. the occupation of the parents. Yet I didn't feel the original info-graphics communicated the multitude of 530 titles.

What are 530 book titles, exactly? 11,197 single characters (letterforms)? Five hours and 23 minutes of copying and pasting? It's all of those things, but I thought it was important to share a more vivid represen-tation of this quantity. I wanted to show what 530 book titles looks like, en masse.

Mimicking Emily's process, which is clearly stated in her text, I logged onto 'Goodreads' and started searching for book titles tagged with 'The' and 'Daughter'. A monotonous task, I decided to make the most of this time and like Emily, I pressed play on a French language podcast I've had on my bucket list for some time. 530 titles later I now know how to introduce myself, make small talk and order a three course meal in French.

Five hours and 23 minutes later I have a heavily populated Excel spreadsheet and a much clearer picture of this title phenomenon. In response, I have produced three new interpre-tations of Emily's research, as well and a fourth infographic which aims to represent the extent of Emily's research and the number of found titles though visual density.

Fig. 1:

Books Titled The ___'s Daughter, 1990–2011

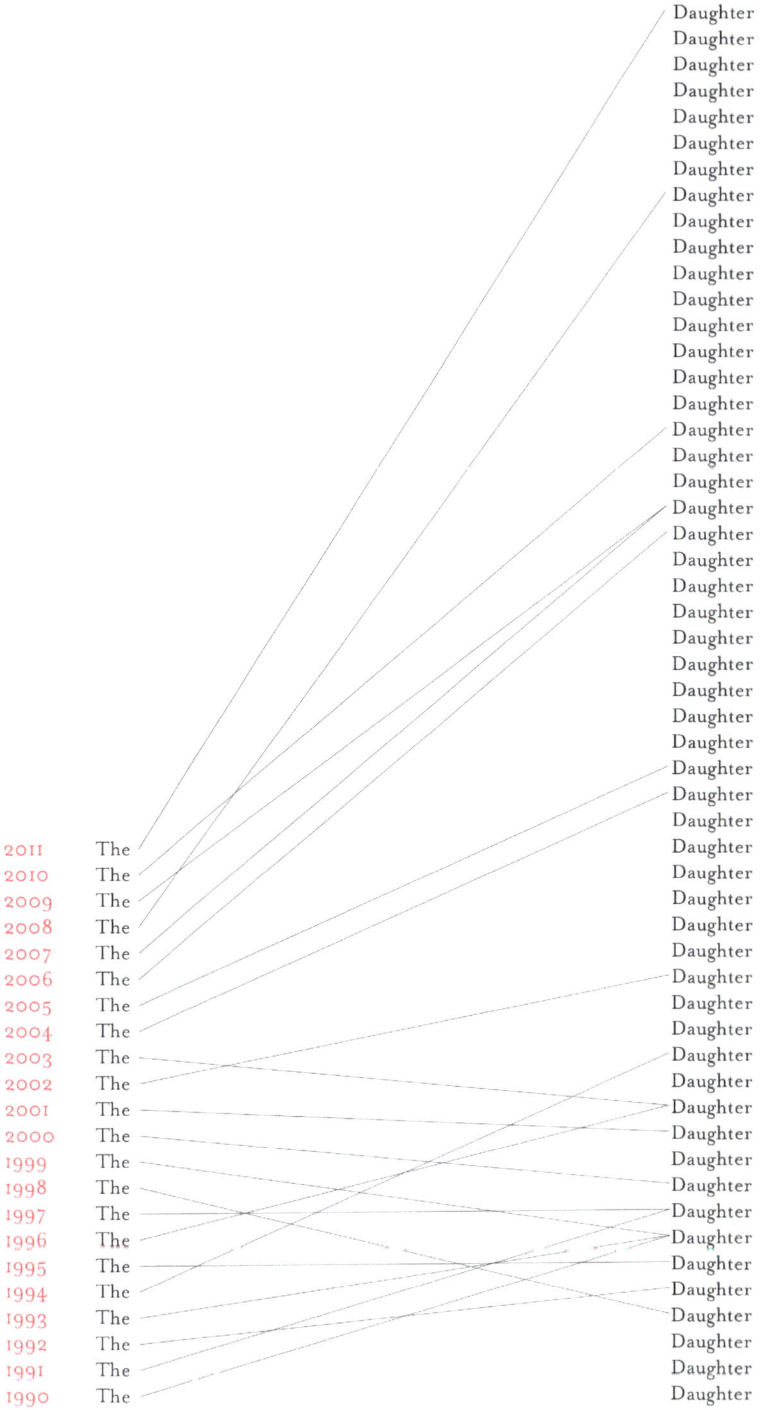

Daughter
Daughter
Daughter
Daughter
Daughter
Daughter
Daughter
Daughter
Daughter
Daughter
Daughter
Daughter
Daughter
Daughter
Daughter
Daughter
Daughter
Daughter
Daughter
Daughter
Daughter
Daughter
Daughter
Daughter
Daughter
Daughter
Daughter
Daughter
Daughter
Daughter
Daughter
Daughter

2011	The	Daughter
2010	The	Daughter
2009	The	Daughter
2008	The	Daughter
2007	The	Daughter
2006	The	Daughter
2005	The	Daughter
2004	The	Daughter
2003	The	Daughter
2002	The	Daughter
2001	The	Daughter
2000	The	Daughter
1999	The	Daughter
1998	The	Daughter
1997	The	Daughter
1996	The	Daughter
1995	The	Daughter
1994	The	Daughter
1993	The	Daughter
1992	The	Daughter
1991	The	Daughter
1990	The	Daughter

MALE

's Daughter – Arley Cole
The Apothecary's Daughter – Patricia Schonstein
The Highwayman's Daughter – Anne Avery
The Rancher's Daughter – Elizabeth Kelly
The Tinker's Daughter – Wendy Lawton
The Nation's Daughter – Valerie Maarten
The Minstrel's Daughter – Linda Smith
The Dictator's Daughter – Lorena Angell
The Vicar's Daughter – Kimberley Comeaux
The Dressmaker's Daughter – Kate Llewellyn
The Bishop's Daughter – Susan Carroll
The Preacher's Daughter – Lyn Cote
The Kingmaker's Daughter – Philippa Wiat
The Shyster's Daughter – Paula Priamos
The Ratcatcher's Daughter – Pamela Rushby
The Spaniard's Daughter – Melanie Gifford
The Enemy's Daughter – Linda Turner
The Traitor's Daughter – Elizabeth Powell
The Butler's Daughter – Joyce Sullivan
The Judge's Daughter – Ruth Hamilton
The Bartender's Daughter – Isabelle Flynn
The Diplomat's Daughter – Liz Crowe
The Saxon's Daughter – Tara O'Dell
The Imam's Daughter – Hannah Shah
The Martian's Daughter – Marina von Neumann Whitman
The Miller's Daughter – Margaret Dickinson
The Postmaster's Daughter – Louis Tracy
The Lightkeeper's Daughter – Paige Winship Dooly
The Stonecutter's Daughter – Janet Woods
The Smuggler's Daughter – Sandra Heath
The Superintendent's Daughter – Marjorie Eccles
The Apothecary's Daughter – Charlotte Betts
The Samurai's Daughter – Lesley Downer
The Admiral's Daughter – Victoria Fyodorova
The Clergyman's Daughter – Julia Jeffries
The Blacksmith's Daughter – Suzanne Adair
The Maid's Daughter – Mary Romero
The Traitor's Daughter – Joanna Makepeace
The Hermit's Daughter – Joan Smith
The Brigadier's Daughter – Catherine March
The Groom's Daughter – Natalie Fox
The Activist's Daughter – Ellyn Bache
The Raider's Daughter – Kimberly Cates
The Mermaid's Daughter – Joyce Gard
The Vicar's Daughter – Deborah Simmons
The Landlord's Daughter – Monica Dickens
The Housekeeper's Daughter – Christine Flynn
The Birdman's Daughter – Cindi Myers
The Soldier's Daughter – Rosie Goodwin
The Beekeeper's Daughter – Janice Carter
The Milliner's Daughter – Charlotte Betts
The Sailmaker's Daughter – Stephanie Johnson
The Wolf's Daughter – Patricia La Barbera
The Liar's Daughter – Laurie Graham
The Pirate's Daughter – Helen Dickson
The Tycoon's Daughter – Caitlyn Duffy

FEMALE

The Torturer's Daughter – Zoe Cannon
The Musician's Daughter – Susanne Dunlap
The Queen's Daughter – Susan Coventry
The Butterfly's Daughter – Mary Alice Monroe
The Florist's Daughter – Patricia Hampl
The Mage's Daughter – Lynn Kurland
The Wizard's Daughter – Barbara Michaels
The President's Daughter – Ellen Emerson White
The Twin's Daughter – Lauren Baratz-Logsted
The Alchemist's Daughter – Mary Lawrence
The Quilter's Daughter – Wanda E. Brunstetter
The Pirate's Daughter – Margaret Cezair-Thompson
The Witch's Daughter – Paula Brackston
The Preacher's Daughter – Beverly Lewis
The Mapmaker's Daughter – Laurel Corona
The President's Daughter – Mariah Stewart
The Bloodletter's Daughter – Linda Lafferty
The Undertaker's Daughter – Kate Mayfield
The Heretic's Daughter – Kathleen Kent
The Frontiersman's Daughter – Laura Frantz
The King's Daughter – Barbara Kyle
The Taxidermist's Daughter – Kate Mosse
The Traitor's Daughter – Paula Brandon
The Detective's Daughter – Lesley Thomson
The Warlord's Daughter – Susan Grant
The Icecutter's Daughter – Tracie Peterson
The Bonesetter's Daughter – Amy Tan
The Heretic's Daughter – Kathleen Kent
The Abortionist's Daughter – Elisabeth Hyde
The Goldsmith's Daughter – Tanya Landman
The King's Daughter – Christie Dickason
The Executioner's Daughter – Jane Hardstaff
The Alchemist's Daughter – Katharine McMahon
The Pitman's Daughter – Marjorie DeLuca
The Macgregor's Daughter – Dee Julian
The Centaur's Daughter – Ellen Jensen Abbott
The Watchmaker's Daughter – Sonia Taitz
The Ambassador's Daughter – Pam Jenoff
The Minister's Daughter – Julie Hearn
The Demon's Daughter – Emma Holly
The Monster's Daughter – Deborah Bryan
The Courtesan's Daughter – Claudia Dain
The Impostor's Daughter – Laurie Sandell
The Astrologer's Daughter – Rebecca Lim
The Courtesan's Daughter – Priscilla Galloway
The Bard's Daughter – Sarah Woodbury
The Lightkeeper's Daughter – Colleen Coble
The Vintner's Daughter – Kristen Harnisch
The Tailor's Daughter – Janice Graham
The Woodsman's Daughter – Gwyn Hyman Rubio
The Apothecary's Daughter – Samantha Jillian Bayarr
The Baker's Daughter – Sarah McCoy
The Dragon's Daughter – Sharon Honeycutt
The Vet's Daughter – Barbara Comyns, Kathryn Davis
The King's Daughter – Caroline Preston
The Bishop's Daughter – Tiffany L. Warren
The Harbormaster's Daughter – Heidi Jon Schmidt
The Dollmaker's Daughters – Dilly Court
The Bookseller's Daughter – Pam Rosenthal
The Gentleman's Daughter – Amanda Vickery
The Apothecary's Daughter – Julie Klassen
The Believer's Daughter – Caitlyn Duffy
The Candidate's Daughter – Kathleen Creighton
The President's Daughter – Barbara Chase-Riboud
The Mortician's Daughter – Elizabeth Bloom
The President's Daughter – Kimberly Brubaker Bradley
The Madman's Daughter – Megan Shepherd
The Gatekeeper's Daughter – Eva Pohler
The Millionaire's Daughter – Dorothy Eden
The Professor's Daughter – Emily Raboteau
The Witch's Daughter – Nina Bawden
The Atheist's Daughter – Renée Harrell
The Cattleman's Daughter – Rachael Treasure
The Lion's Daughter – Loretta Chase
The Dowager's Daughter – Mona Prevel
The Demon's Daughter – Paula Altenburg
The Vicar's Daughter – Betty Neels
The Hustler's Daughter – Pinky Dior
The Preacher's Daughter – Cheryl St.John
The Virgin's Daughter – Laura Andersen
The Devil's Daughter – Suzie Grant
The King's Daughter – Sandra Worth
The Doctor's Daughter – Amy Blizzard
The Alpha's Daughter – Jacqueline Rhoades
The Viscount's Daughter – Caitlyn Duffy
The Senator's Daughter – Victoria Gotti
The Storyteller's Daughter – Saira Shah
The Spymaster's Daughter – Jeane Westin
The Shopkeeper's Daughter – Lily Baxter
The Doctor's Daughter – Hilma Wolitzer
The Bearwalker's Daughter – Beth Trissel
The Pinata-Maker's Daughter – Eileen Granfors
The Keeper's Daughter – Gill Arbuthnott
The Tutor's Daughter – Julie Klassen
The Poacher's Daughter – Mary Nichols
The Bearkeeper's Daughter – Gillian Bradshaw
The Executioner's Daughter – Laura E. Williams
The Parson's Daughter – Catherine Cookson
The Shogun's Daughter – Laura Joh Rowland
The Duke's Daughter – Angela Thirkell
The Warrior's Daughter – Holly Bennett
The Doctor's Daughter – Belle Blackburn
The Tsarina's Daughter – Carolly Erickson
The Warlock's Daughter – Jennifer Blake
The Painter's Daughter – Julie Klassen
The Pope's Daughter – Caroline P. Murphy
The Highwayman's Daughter – Henriette Gyland
The Sheriff's Daughter – Kay Stockham
The Colonel's Daughter – Lili Tufel
The Coven's Daughter – Lucy Jago
The Cartographer's Daughter – Karen L. Abrahamson
The Billionaire's Daughter – Maggie Carpenter
The Quack's Daughter – Greta Nettleton
The Traitor's Daughter – Barbara Kyle
The Devil's Daughter – Laura Drewry
The Miller's Daughter – Emile Zola
The Maid's Daughter – Janice Maynard
The Colonel's Daughter – Rose Tremain
The Mapmaker's Daughter – Caroline Dunford
The Caretaker's Daughter – Gabrielle Goldsby
The Doctor's Daughter – Judith Bowen
The Pornographer's Daughter – Kristin Battista-Frazee
The Eagle's Daughter – Judith Tarr
The Artist's Daughter – Kimiko Hahn
The Officer's Daughter – Zina Rohan
The Innkeeper's Daughter – Val Wood

Fig. 2:
Is the author of The ___'s Daughter a man or a woman?

Fig. 3
Who are her parents?

Probably unmarried

Keepers of inns / lighthouses

Law enforcement / judiciary

Pseudo-sciencey things

In retail

Medically inclined

Possibly metaphorical

Work with animals

Military

Laborers

Villainous

Involved with the Church

In Politics

Magical / Supernatural

Connected to Royalty

Artists or Artisans

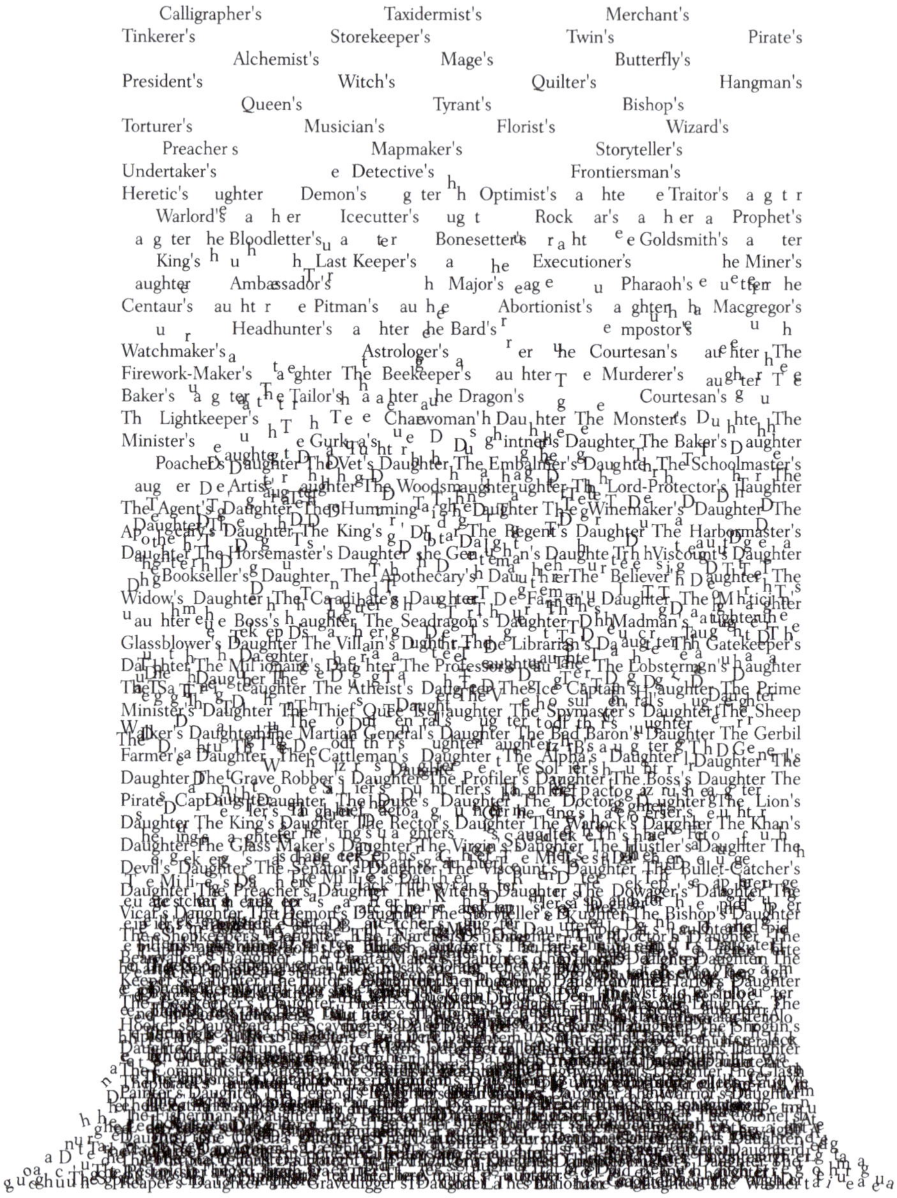

Calligrapher's Taxidermist's Merchant's
Tinkerer's Storekeeper's Twin's Pirate's
Alchemist's Mage's Butterfly's
President's Witch's Quilter's Hangman's
Queen's Tyrant's Bishop's
Torturer's Musician's Florist's Wizard's
Preacher s Mapmaker's Storyteller's
Undertaker's e Detective's Frontiersman's

Fig. 4:
530 instances of books titled 'The ___'s Daughter.'
Source: www.goodreads.com

Artist's Musician's Leopard's Quack's
King's Enchanter's Unicorn's
Giant's Preacher's Traitor's Tamer's
Zookeeper's Moneylender's
Maid's Colonel's Caretaker's Mapmaker's
u ter Captain's e h Cantor's a r e Undertaker's u h er he
Doctor's au hter T Fire i g's ug ter Kingmaker's a r e Traitor's
a gh er h Legate's a ghter Runner's au ht r h Pornographer's u er
T e Dreamthief's aughter he Killer's a gh er a e d t g Preacher's ht r
h Eagle's a g te Monk n Hangman's au h er e Alchemist's aug ter
Rodeo Man's a u hter e President's aughter T e Man's D u hter The
Mistress's Daughter e Piano au ter he Officer's a h er The Innkeeper's
Da h er The Viking's D ghter T Bookie's a g e e Blacksmith's ug ter The
Goldsmith's Daughter The Sin-Eater's Daughter The Pope's aughter h Sovereign's
Daughter The King's Daughter The Sorcerer's Daughter The Century's D g ter T e Marsh
King's Daughter The Bookmaker's aughter The Stonekeeper's Daughter The Candidate's
Daughter The Sultan's Daughter The Tree Shepherd's Daughter The Apothecary's Da gh er
The Rancher's Daughter The Nation's Daughter T h Dictato 's aughter The Tinker's
Daughter The Highwayman's Daughter The Minstrel's Daughter The Dressmaker's
Daughter The Cartel's Daughter The Kingmaker's aughter The Rabbi's aughter The
Tarot Reader's Dau hter The Shyster's Daughter The Traitor's Daughter The Bishop's
Daughter The Vicar's Daughter The Mayor's aughter The Blacksmith's Daughter The
Captain's Daughter The Samurai's Daughter The Preacher's Daughter The Fat M n's
Daughter The Spaniard's Daughter The Enemy's Daughter The Sergeant Major's Dau hter
The Judge's Daughter The Ripper's Daughter The Spider King's Daughter The Bart nder's
Daughter The High King's Daughter The Commodore's Daughter The Diplomat's Daughter
The Blacksmith's Daughter The Ratcatcher's Daughter The Miller's Daughter The Imam's
Daughter The Lightkeeper's Daughter The Butler's Daughter The Lace Maker's Daughter
The Martian's Daughter The Postmaster's Daughter The Fortune Teller's Daughter The
Saxon's Daughter The Demon Count's Daughter The Stonecutter's Daughter The Teacher's
Daughter The Farmer's Daughter The King's Daughter The Smuggler's Daughter The
Astrologer's Daughter The Superintendent's Daughter The Apothecary's Daughter The
Samurai's Daughter The Chief Inspector's Daughter The Superstar's Daughter The
Admiral's Daughter The Admiral's Daughter The Millionaire's Daughter The Clergyman's
Daughter The Blacksmith's Daughter The Shopkeeper's Daughter The Faun and the
Woodcutter's Daughter The King's Daughters The Snake Catcher's Daughter The Maid's
Daughter The Ambassador's Daughter The Alchemist's Daughter The Traitor's Daughter
The Magician's Daughter The Hermit's Daughter The Brigadier's Daughter The Regent's
Daughter The Wolf's Daughter The Woman's Daughter The Groom's Daughter The
Activist's Daughter The General's Daughter The Raider's Daughter The Shell Lady's
Daughter The Colonel's Daughter The Minister's Daughter The Mermaid's Daughter The
Egyptian Demon's Daughter The Lighthouse Keeper's Daughter The Surgeon's Daughter
The Admiral's Daughter The Vicar's Daughter The Rustler's Daughter The Landlord's
[illegible]

43

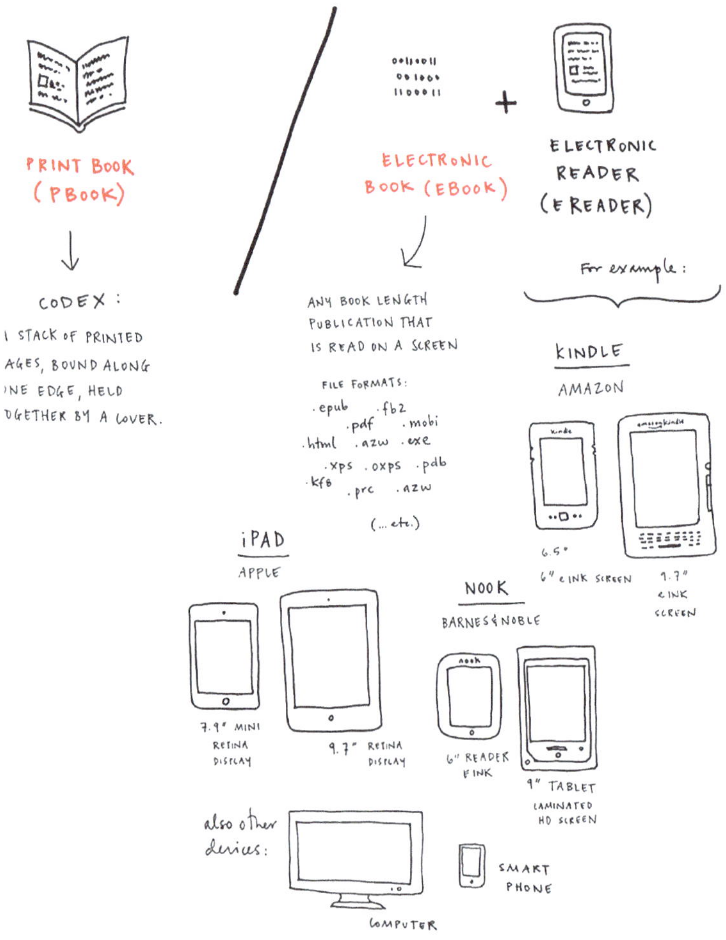

PRINT BOOK (PBOOK)

CODEX:

I STACK OF PRINTED
AGES, BOUND ALONG
NE EDGE, HELD
OGETHER BY A COVER.

ELECTRONIC BOOK (EBOOK)

0011001
001000
1100011

ANY BOOK LENGTH PUBLICATION THAT IS READ ON A SCREEN

FILE FORMATS:

.epub .fb2 .pdf .mobi .html .azw .exe .xps .oxps .pdb .kf8 .prc .azw

(... etc.)

\+ ELECTRONIC READER (EREADER)

For example:

KINDLE

AMAZON

6.5"

6" e INK SCREEN

9.7" e INK SCREEN

iPAD

APPLE

7.9" MINI RETINA DISPLAY

9.7" RETINA DISPLAY

NOOK

BARNES & NOBLE

6" READER E INK

9" TABLET LAMINATED HD SCREEN

also other devices:

COMPUTER

SMART PHONE

'P-BOOK *vs.* E-BOOK' ILLUSTRATION

by ZOË SADOKIERSKI

pBooks, eBooks and dBooks:

Why we are hooked on bookishness.

An excerpt.

TOM UGLOW

—

Originally published December 22 2014:
medium.com/@tomux

—

ARCHITECTS OF READING
4:30 – 5:30PM, SAT. 23 MAY
PHILHARMONIA STUDIO
HICKSON RD, WALSH BAY

TOM UGLOW
I work for Google, but the rest of the time I'm a mumbling creative prone to tangents, prosopagnasia, declamation and technobibliophilism

I KNOW THAT READING is not the same as *reading*. I can watch TV and read, but I cannot read and watch TV. In fact when I am immersed in reading, when I am inside a thriller, or a history, or a neo-gothic fairy tale then I am catatonic. I could be anywhere, and I cannot do anything else, I cannot talk, text, tweet. (I can listen to music but somehow one doesn't *hear* the music). Sometimes I walk and read—a habit we all hate in others—but, I can't *really* read and walk. And, when I look up from a period of *reading* it is like coming out of water, suddenly all the sounds of the world descend and I see the people and the traffic and the noise of the real world around me. Does that sound familiar?

That's what reading means to me. The last few weeks I have been reading *The Children's Book*, by AS Byatt. Every day I sit in the park and get twenty minutes alone in her world, a different, Victorian time, among a lavishly detailed cast of souls. I have recently taken to reading books on my phone (a Nexus 5). To be honest I find this behaviour somewhat scandalous, yet there I am, swiping page after page, rattling through fairy kingdoms and lustful teenage yearnings, thinking about reading. So I started to make a list called: Why are digital books good?

Why are eBooks good?

I scratched out ~~digital~~ because the word 'digital' means something different to me. Why are eBooks good? Let's run through the positives. Starting with:

All books are good.

But beyond that:

1. eBooks are light; of infinite capacity; readable; unloseable; searchable; scaleable; unbreakable; untearable; easy to read in the dark; hard to read in bright light; (reverse that for Kindles); they are in your pocket/bag always; they are easy to find; simple to buy; they don't get mouldy, wet and they don't fall apart. They are really easy.

2. Things they will be: shareable; collaborative; unbound to time or geography creating multimedia, interactive, co-reading experiences across distances; they could be extraordinary.

3. eBooks mean that you can be a thousand miles from a bookshelf and carry the Booker Prize longlist in your pocket.

eBooks have transformed lives, and that definitely rates as 'good'.

What is a book?

I did a masters in book art, at Camberwell College—making elaborate, quirky, very physical books—so that may colour my views. Additionally in this essay I'm talking about particular genres—novels, poetry, history, biography, popular science and current affairs—not manuals or text-books, recipes or maps. In this sense, to me a book is an experience that you lose yourself in reading: what we could call its 'immersive' quality. The magic part. And we can time-travel on a Kindle just as easily as a paperback. (Jeanette Winterson recently spoke amazingly on this quality.) We have our favourite literary landscapes, we have visions that were etched in young minds and inspire for a lifetime. And if you are reading this, I'm sure like me you have experienced many moments of looking up from a book and waking as if from a dream. It's an Infinite List: whether histories (Beevor, Mantel) or cartoons (Ware), mathematicians (du Sautoy) and novelists (Pynchon, Pullman, Pratchett), not to mention anything by Robert Harris (for which I have a shockingly soft spot). It is hard to define this magic bookness. Sometimes I think it is about the form; sometimes about the words, certainly it is psychological, words are isolating and unavoid-ably meaning-full: but magic is not held in the form of e-reader, phone or paper.

Generically and traditionally books are been primarily static (they don't change much) and they follow some loose patterns:

— *Books are generally textual and live in the reader's mind's eye rather than pre-constructed (e.g. video or games), although it may have pictures and typographic play (but this is less usual).*

— *Conventionally, books present a paginal narrative; or, if not paginal, linear; or, if not linear, a multi-dimensional self-contained reality: a 'world' of the authors imagination. See Tolkein, or Rowling; or Dahl, Defoe or Dickens, or any good author, or even a bad one.*

— *Temporality has no place in books. Decades may pass in a sentence, or seconds in chapters.*

All of this happens equally well on OLED as it does on pulp or vellum.

What is wonderful about the physical book?

1. Paper is nice.
2. Data gets lost.
3. Digital is like latin.
4. Physical is tactile.

The fact that we still love the book-as-a-book may simply be to do with its own physicality. The sensual appeal of a book in the hand. It's nice to imagine for a moment the pen, hovering over a blank, thin-ruled page, and watch words emerge from puddles of ink, bleeding down crushed valleys of fine wood pulp, letter-pressing dreams and layering meaning on inference on innuendo into the leathery, well-thumbed leaves. Imagine we stripped away all of that: the penciled annotations, my scrawled marginalia, the coffee ring, the folds, the ink, the errors, lines of struck through text, and the trace memories of reading and re-reading, of written words pronounced out loud. What would be left? Even a few scraps clipped together has form, it becomes fleshed out and present. It is more real to us—and there is a reason for that.

Words on paper have body language and meaning, they hold a library of information that we don't see or understand: a history of metadata that we cannot parse.

And yet, if you were reading this in a digital format you could access it anywhere, carry it without weight, share it, lose it, and, most of all, you could look at it on your phone. It is easy.

By the way, easy doesn't make it digital. I don't quite understand why an electronic book is described as digital, when it is no more digital than my TV, and significantly less digital than my phone. Neither of them get a 'digital' prefix. Indeed neither do I call it my 'electronic telly'. These are books. As paperbacks are to hardbacks these new books are pixelbacks. All have their place.

Paper is nice. We mark our books. And they mark us back, they write notes in our margins, they fold over corners of our psyche—we will never escape the cumulative effect of our reading. Sometimes it is good to have a receipt of that journey.

TOP:
Tom's physical library

BOTTOM:
Tom's digital library

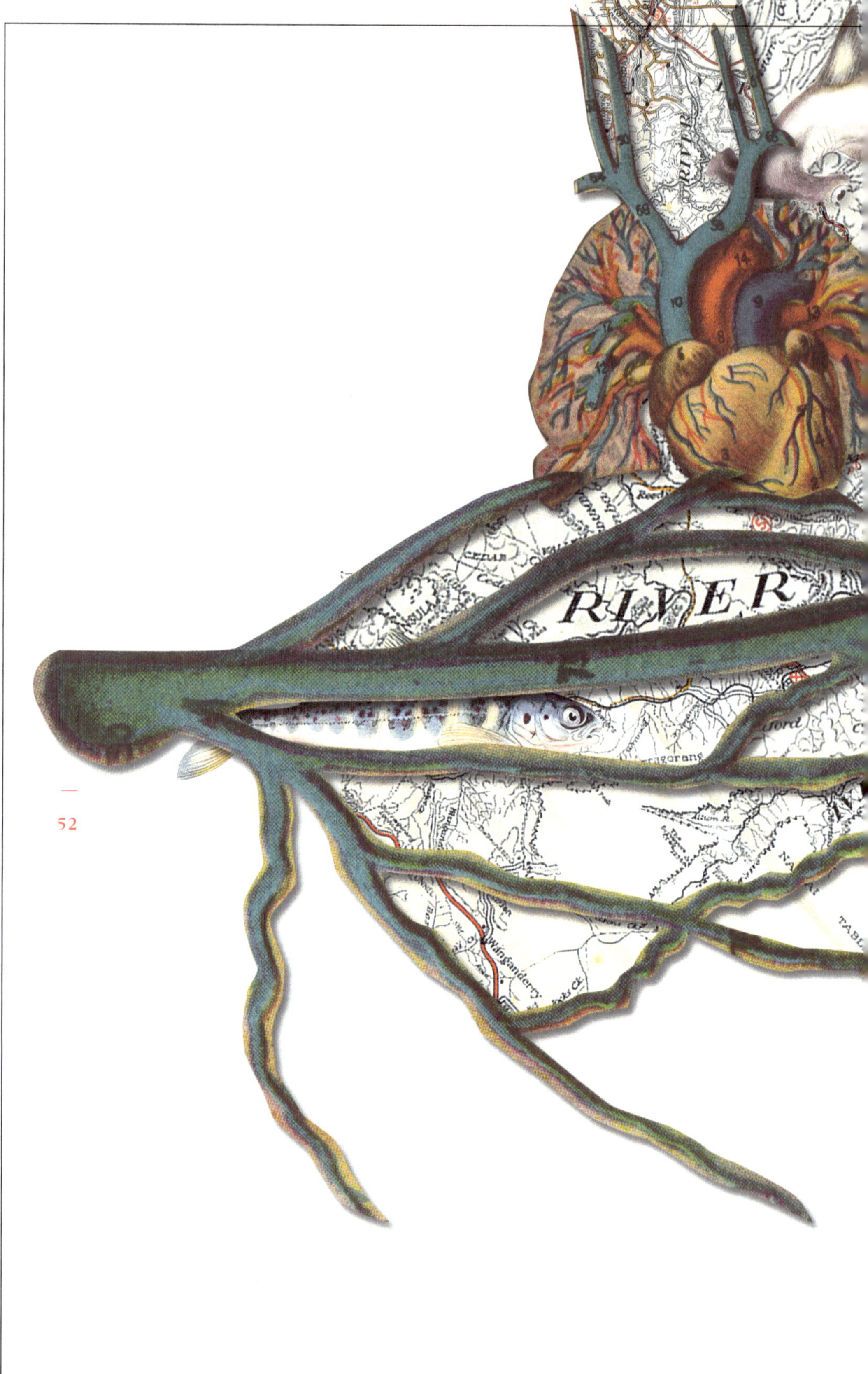
RIVER

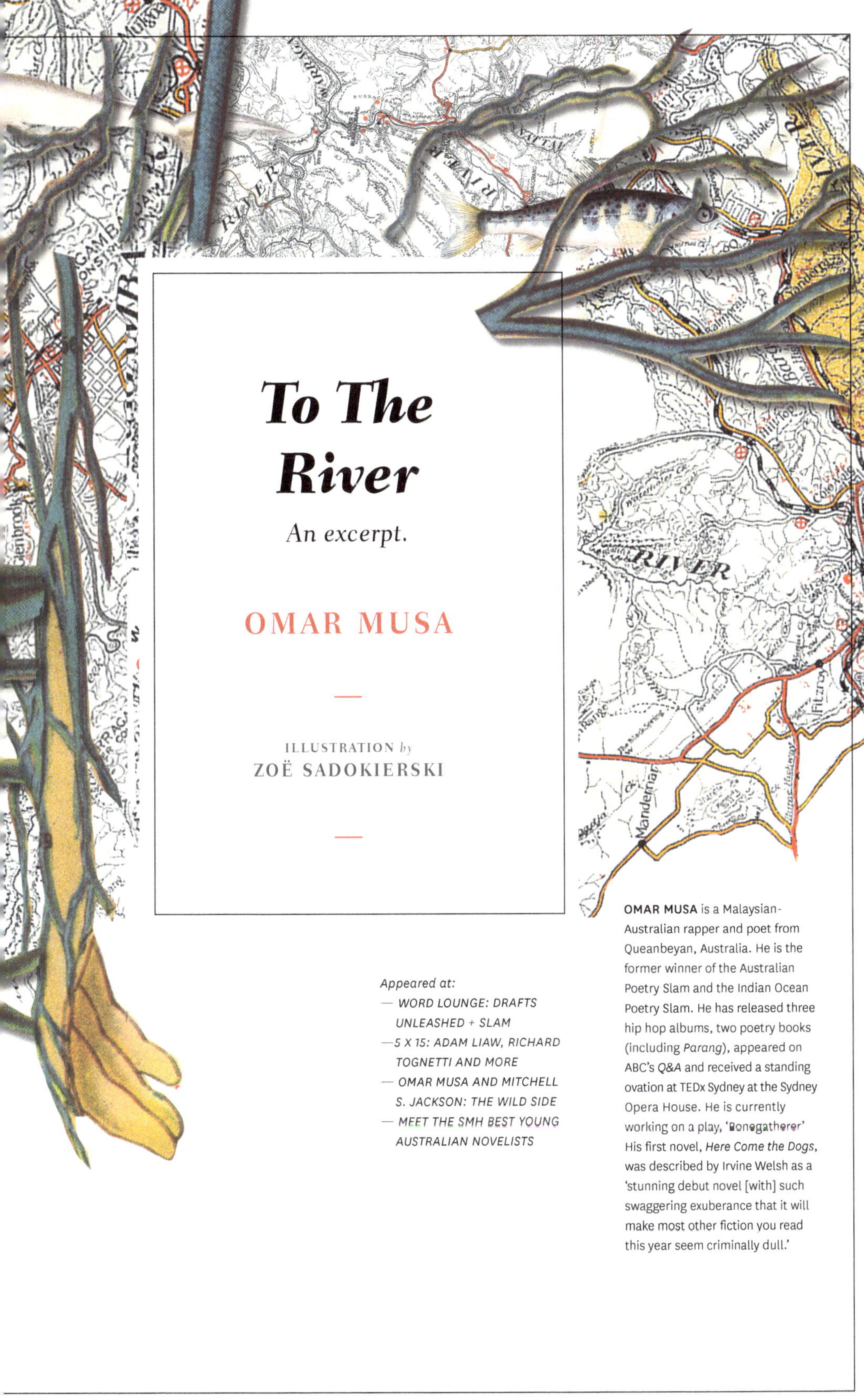

To The River

An excerpt.

OMAR MUSA

—

ILLUSTRATION *by*
ZOË SADOKIERSKI

—

Appeared at:

- *WORD LOUNGE: DRAFTS UNLEASHED + SLAM*
- *5 X 15: ADAM LIAW, RICHARD TOGNETTI AND MORE*
- *OMAR MUSA AND MITCHELL S. JACKSON: THE WILD SIDE*
- *MEET THE SMH BEST YOUNG AUSTRALIAN NOVELISTS*

OMAR MUSA is a Malaysian-Australian rapper and poet from Queanbeyan, Australia. He is the former winner of the Australian Poetry Slam and the Indian Ocean Poetry Slam. He has released three hip hop albums, two poetry books (including *Parang*), appeared on ABC's *Q&A* and received a standing ovation at TEDx Sydney at the Sydney Opera House. He is currently working on a play, 'Bonegatherer' His first novel, *Here Come the Dogs*, was described by Irvine Welsh as a 'stunning debut novel [with] such swaggering exuberance that it will make most other fiction you read this year seem criminally dull.'

WHEN I WAS YOUNG, I could smell The River from my bedroom window. It was as if its muscular brown body had uncoiled and was moving its silent force through the air towards me. Sometimes, rain comes down the steep slopes of the Gourock Range and the Tinderry Mountains, feeding The River, engorging it so that it rises dark and steady, taking hold of the banks and the roads, up up over the low bridge leading into Oaks Estate, up up over the Morrisset Bridge, up up up flattening out the willows and blackberry bushes, smelling of wood-rot and redfin, sounding like thunder and threat, promise and a lost past.

The River — named for its clear waters, axe country, flint country, water gum-hickory—ti tree country, wallaroo, brolga, emu-opossum skin-corroboree country, where later the pit-saw and adze built huts of hardwood and stringbark, where nuns tip-toed across stones from one bank to the other, only a few miles from where Austrians and Germans were interned during World War I. The River — where teenagers suck, fuck and smoke in Fairmonts and Falcons, where dudes with Aussie Pride tatts on the backs of their hands, sip without pride on Woodstock cans.

Once in The River's braided body there were Murray cod, Macquarie perch, golden and silver, so numerous that it was first named The Fish River. So numerous that back in the early days, floods scattered fish over the streets of Queanbeyan, as if pieces of the moon had fallen, bending and dancing over the dusty macadam. You won't find many Murray cod in The River any more. Now, young fellas named Corey and Nathan and Rhys catch four kilo carp with corn cobs on running sinker rigs. Tailings from the mine in Captain's Flat ruined the waters long ago, full as they are of rusted trolleys and sometimes bodies, floating with suburban jellyfish, discarded rubber remnants of midnight follies.

When I was a child, my parents warned me about The River, because tigersnakes bit children and dogs there. When I was a child, an old blackfella saved me from drowning, hoisting me up from the water, with strong, tobacco-scented hands in my armpits.

Photo Credit: William Yang

Robert Adamson and Juno Gemes.

Launch of *The Clean Dark*, the Dixon Room, State Library of New South Wales. 1990.

PHOTOGRAPHER: William Yang

Garden Poem

ROBERT ADAMSON

for Juno

PHOTO ILLUSTRATION
'MANDALA FOR MARGARET OLLEY'
Created 2013, the year Garden Poem was written.

JUNO GEMES

Poem originally published in
Net Needle, 2015

POETRY AND MUSIC SALON: POETRY VS PROSE
WITH ***Robert Adamson, Minah Choe, Stephen Edgar, Luke Fischer, Goetz Richter and Melinda Smith***

4:30–6:00PM, SAT. MAY 23
SYDNEY DANCE LOUNGE,
HICKSON RD, WALSH BAY

ROBERT ADAMSON is the author of *Net Needle*. His previous collection of poetry was *The Golden Bird*, which won the CJ Dennis Prize for Poetry in the 2009 Victorian Premier's Literary Awards. He has published numerous volumes of poetry in Australia and overseas. His memoir, *Inside Out*, was shortlisted for *The Age* Book of the Year Award. He edited *The Best Australian Poems* 2009 and 2010.

Sunlight scatters wild bees across a blanket
of flowering lavender. The garden

grows, visibly, in one morning—
native grasses push up, tough and lovely

as your angel's trumpets. At midday
the weather, with bushfire breath, walks about

talking to itself. A paper wasp zooms
above smooth river pebbles. In the trees

possums lie flat on leafy branches to cool off,
the cats notice, then fall back to sleep.

This day has taken our lives to arrive.
Afternoon swings open, although

the mechanics of the sun require
the moon's white oil. Daylight fades to twilight

streaking bottlebrush flowers with shade,
a breeze clatters in the green bamboo and shakes

its lank hair. At dinnertime, the French doors present us
with a slice of night, shining clear—

a Naples yellow moon outlines the ridges
of the mountains—all this, neatly laid out

on the dining room table
across patches of moonlight.

ILLUSTRATION *by*
OLIVIA KING

Questions on happiness

REBECCA HUNTLEY

THE HAPPINESS DILEMMA
10:00 – 11:00AM
SUN. MAY 24
PIER 2/3 MAIN STAGE
HICKSON ROAD
WALSH BAY

In which Rebecca Huntley asked Matt Haig, Paul Dolan, Amanda Lohrey if happiness really is what it's all about.

—

What makes you happy? How did you discover the secret to your own happiness? How old were you when you worked it out?

Is the opposite of depression happiness?

Can you tell someone who is clinically depressed they will be happy one day? Is that possible?

Lots of creative and famous people have been famously and creatively depressed. Matt Haig says, 'depression makes thinkers out of all of us'. Did you ever worry that if you were happy you'd be a less interesting writer?

What can we learn about happiness from Buddhism even if we don't want to be a Buddhist?

REBECCA HUNTLEY is a social researcher, writer and broadcaster with a PhD in gender studies. For nearly nine years she was the executive director of The Mind & Mood Report. She was a feature writer for *Vogue*, a columnist for *BRW* and the presenter of RN Drive on a Friday. She co-presents a weekly podcast with Sarah McDonald, *Just Between Us*. She is the author of numerous books, the latest entitled *Does Cooking Matter?*

Rebecca also appeared at:
— In the Age of Google, What's the Point of Schools?
— Anna Bligh: Through the Wall
— Michael Cooney: The Gillard Project

Appeared at:

— *DRAWING CHARACTERS: BODY LANGUAGE AND GESTURES*

— *FAMILY DAY EVENTS: CHALK ART ILLUSTRATOR BATTLE ROUNDS*

Award-winning artist **TONY FLOWERS** is the illustrator of *Saurus Street*, a six-book adventure series about a normal everyday street that attracts unusual, dinosaur-shaped visitors. Tony has worked on educational, chapter and picture books in Australia and has a Masters degree in visual communication. His most highly valued prize to date has been from the Oshima Picture Book Museum in Toyama, Japan, for his hand made pop-up book.

ILLUSTRATION by

TONY FLOWERS

at The Book of Days workstation

OLD TOM
HORRIBLE HARRIET
& MR Chicken ..

LeighHOBBS.

At the SWF the creator crushed by his creations.

ILLUSTRATION by

LEIGH HOBBS

at The Book of Days workstation

APPEARED AT:
— FAMILY DAY: DRAW ALONG WITH LEIGH HOBBS (MAY 24)
— PRIMARY SCHOOL DAYS IN: PARRAMATTA (MAY 18); CITY (MAY 19 + 20); FREE AT TOWN HALL (MAY 21); PENRITH (MAY 23).

LEIGH HOBBS works across a wide range of artistic mediums, but is best known for his children's books featuring Old Tom, Horrible Harriet, Mr Badger and Mr Chicken. *Mr Chicken Goes to Paris* was shortlisted for the Prime Minister's Literary Awards and the CBCA Awards, and is a bestseller at Paris's Louvre Bookstore. Since childhood, Leigh's had a passion for art, architecture, classical music, English history ... and London, a place he finds endlessly fascinating and visits regularly. He admits there's something of himself in each of his characters and says his most recent book, *Mr Chicken Lands on London*, could, in a way, be seen as a love story.

Elain Richards, Dymocks

Forest for the Trees:

Writers & Publishing *in* 2015

10:00 AM - 4:30 PM
THURSDAY, MAY 21

STATE LIBRARY OF NSW,
METCALFE AUDITORIUM,
MACQUARIE ST, SYDNEY

PRESENTED WITH THE
NSW WRITERS' CENTRE

ILLUSTRATIONS DRAWN LIVE *by*
LEIGH RIGOZZI

Cat Sparks

The cure for dry elbows is stickytaping avocado skins to them.

Walter Mason

Ash Davies, Tablo

Bringing together writers, publishers and industry representatives, this one-day seminar explored the state of writing and publishing in Australia. This was the program of events:

MY PATH THROUGH THE FOREST
10:00 — 10:45am

A writer's life entails much more than just getting words on the page. Bruce McCabe self-published his first novel, *Skinjob*, which led to an international publishing deal with Random House. He takes us through what he learned and his plans for 2015.

A FORK IN THE ROAD
10:45 – 11:30AM

Bruce McCabe is joined by Sophie Masson, award-winning author of more than 60 books for children, young adults and adults, to discuss the many pathways to publication. This is an opportunity to ask these successful authors, with very different experiences, about what they've learnt, and what they would and wouldn't recommend.

HUNTING AND GATHERING – WHAT CAN DATA TELL US?
11:45AM – 12:45PM

What does the data say, who is collecting it and how do we interpret it? What do we know about readers? Who reads? On what platforms? Are ebooks really 30 per cent of the market? Shaun Symonds, General Manager, Nielsen BookScan; John Purcell, Head of Marketing, Booktopia; and Elain Richards, Loyalty & Marketing Manager, Dymocks in conversation with Mark Higginson, mPath Consulting.

PLANTING THE SEED
12:45 – 1:45PM

Four authors talk social media and debate the pros and cons of various platforms. Walter Mason (*Destination Cambodia*) chirps up for Twitter, Jan Cornall (*Take Me to Paradise*) advocates for email lists, A.L. Tait (*The Mapmaker Chronicles*) 'likes' Facebook and Kylie Scott (*The Stage Dive Series*) pins Pinterest.

TO MARKET, TO MARKET
2:30 – 3:30PM

How do publishers identify the target audience for a book and how do they make sure books and readers find each other? Hear how decisions are made on everything from acquisition through to marketing, with Kate Cuthbert, Managing Editor, Escape Publishing, Anna Valdinger, Fiction Publisher, HarperCollins and Aviva Tuffield, Publisher, Affirm Press.

THE OPEN ROAD
3:30 – 4:30PM

What are the new opportunities for getting your work out to audiences (and getting paid)? This panel explores new platforms (audio books, social reading), sales models (subscriptions and bundling), revenue streams, and much more. Author, editor, and blogger Angela Meyer talks to Joel Naoum, Momentum; Malcolm Neil, Kobo; Cat Sparks (*The Bride Prince*) and Ash Davies, Tablo.

Allison Tait

Angela Meyer

Bruce McCabe at Forest for the Trees.

Sophie Masson
at Forest for the Trees

John Purcell, Booktopia

Aviva Tuffield
~~Anna Valdinger~~

Mark Higginson
mPath consulting

Jan Cornall

YAN QIN WENG

'GRASSLAND'

from the Ex Libris series, 2012

SELECTED
Curiosity Lectures

HOSTED BY
DAMON YOUNG

'An intellectual yum cha offering audiences a taste of varied ideas: dinosaurs and cinema, archaeology of Cambodia (and climate change), pandemics, non-monogamy, Elvis's hips and the primal in music and more. Festival-goers could drop into the Pier 2/3 stage, grab a coffee or wine and nibble on facts, theories, impressions and stories.'

— www.damonyoung.com.au

Dr **DAMON YOUNG** is a philosopher and writer. He is the author of *Distraction*, *Philosophy in the Garden*, and the recently published *How to Think About Exercise*. His books have been published in Australia and abroad, and translated into various languages including Italian, Spanish, Dutch, Turkish and Korean. Damon is also the author of two children's books: *My Nanna is a Ninja* and *My Pop is a Pirate*. He recently won the AAP media prize for his work as a public intellectual.

Damon also appeared at:
— FAMILY DAY: ENID BLYTON STORYTIME CLUBHOUSE

FULL CURIOSITY PROGRAM:

THURS. MAY 21

LESLEY CHAMBERLAIN:
ON THE STORY OF VAN GOGH'S SHOES

REBECCA SHEEHAN:
ON POP

FRANK BRENNAN:
ON A MEDDLING WHITEFELLA

HARRISON YOUNG:
ON BEING SURPRISED

JOHN PICKRELL:
ON THE PROBLEMS WITH JURASSIC PARK

ANDREW FORD:
ON ELVIS'S HIPS

KAREN HITCHCOCK:
ON OLD AGE

FRI.MAY 22

NICHOLAS JOSE:
ON FORTUNE

ROLAND FLETCHER:
ON PAST FUTURES

ZOË SADOKIERSKI:
ON READING WITH OUR HANDS

JANE DE TELIGA:
ON RUNNING AWAY FROM HOME

ANNE MANNE:
ON NARCISSISM

JAMES BOYCE:
ON HOW ORIGINAL SIN MADE THE WEST

LEE KOFMAN:
ON NON-MONOGAMY

SAT. MAY 23

CAROLINE OVERINGTON:
ON CAPITAL PUNISHMENT

ROBERT DESSAIX:
ON HOW ENID BLYTON CHANGED MY LIFE

FIONA ALLON:
ON HIPSTERS

DENNIS ALTMAN:
ON QUER[Y]ING AGATHA CHRISTIE

JANE GLEESON-WHITE:
ON WHY ACCOUNTANTS MIGHT SAVE THE PLANET

EMILY ST JOHN MANDEL:
ON PANDEMICS

KÁRI GÍSLASON:
ON MEETING VIKING ANCESTORS

CORONA
AGATHA CHRISTIE
REMINGTON PORTABLE No. 2
REMINGTON PORTABLE No. 5
CORONA
REMINGTONS
REMINGTON RAND

Quer[y]ing Agatha Christie

An excerpt.

DENNIS ALTMAN

—

An ironic and affectionate take on Agatha Christie, the most read mystery writer of all time.

—

ON QUER[Y]ING AGATHA CHRISTIE
1.30 – 2.10PM, SAT. MAY 23
PIER 2/3 CURIOSITY STAGE
HICKSON RD, WALSH BAY

ALSO APPEARED AT:
— THE COLD WAR ON SEX

DENNIS ALTMAN is a professorial fellow in human security at LaTrobe University, is the author of twelve influential books, including *Homosexual: Oppression & Liberation*, *AIDS and the New Puritanism*, *Global Sex*, and *Gore Vidal's America*. *The Bulletin* listed Dennis Altman as one of the 100 most influential Australians in 2006, and he was appointed a Member of the Order of Australia. *The End of the Homosexual?* summarises changes in our understandings and perceptions of homosexuality over 40 years, both locally and globally.

Originally published 5 January 2009
Inside Story: www.insidestory.org.au

ILLUSTRATION *by*
ZOË SADOKIERSKI

AGATHA CHRISTIE was a shared passion with my friend, the poet Dorothy Porter, who died last month, and it is partly in her memory that I am writing this piece. 'Which Aggie are you reading now?' Dorothy would ask when we met and then tell me about the one currently on her bedside table. Some years ago we did a joint presentation to the Melbourne chapter of Sisters in Crime on 'Queering Agatha'.

Agatha Christie seems to have timeless appeal. If you associate her with nostalgia for a lost Gilbert and Sullivan, pearl necklace and sherry drinking middle England, try giving her books to a smart ten year old. I lent several of my Christies to one, who was particularly taken by the sleight of hand Christie uses in *Death in the Clouds*.

Partly through movie adaptations, of which there are around thirty, but also through the enthusiasm of readers, some of her books have become staples of twentieth century fiction: who has not heard of Miss Marple and Hercule Poirot, or been caught up in the sheer ingenuity of plotting in books like *Murder on the Orient Express*, *The Murder of Roger Ackroyd* or *Then There Were None* (originally *Ten Little Niggers*, then briefly, before that too was recognised as offensive, *Ten Little Indians*)?

It is commonplace to argue that Christie was a bad writer, and she pales beside the best of her successors, including P. D. James, Ruth Rendell and Elizabeth George. Her dialogue is wooden, her characters one dimensional, her language appropriate to the uneducated for whom she expressed such contempt. She was a snob and a racist: the casual anti-Semitism of 1930s England runs through her early novels, in almost all of which there are minor Jewish characters, usually identified by avarice and physical appearance: 'men of Hebraic extraction, sallow men with hooked noses, wearing flamboyant jewellery.' Christie had no compunction in saying she disliked 'Negroes,' and south Asians and Africans only appear in classic colonial guise in her books; note the contempt for 'the natives' viewed from the boat in *Death on the Nile*. She seems to have had a low opinion of Australians, too, though (white) South Africans and Canadians fare better.

We read Christie despite her prejudices, not because of them, just as one might enjoy James Bond as entertainment but deplore Fleming's sexism and love of violence. To take her too seriously—to quote the praise of Roland Barthes, Umberto Eco and Michel Houllebecq—is to fall into the same trap that allows French critics to see profundities in the films of Jerry Lewis. Sometimes the superficial is all there is.

YOU CAN ONLY READ Christie as 'queer'—as Dorothy and I did at Sisters in Crime—if you accept that this as a game in which both the genre and the theory are being read ironically. Even with the insouciance that typifies queer theorists there is no reason to believe that Christie herself was sexually attracted to women. But her novels are full of unmarried men and spinster women—both Marple and Poirot are unattached with only vague hints of failed romance in a long past life—and, as Dorothy remarked, remarkably free of children, who are often unpleasant when they do appear.

It's not difficult to find coded homosexual references in Christie, particularly in her novels set in English villages where single artistic men and devoted women companions abound. In *A Murder is Announced*, for instance, there is an obvious lesbian couple. In one of her later books *Nemesis* a lesbian relationship lies behind the murder itself, a theme Ruth Rendell used in one of her early novels *From Doon With Death*. At least one of her minor detectives, Mr Sattherwaite, cries out for a queer reading: what is to make of a man who 'is an admirer of Kew Gardens and was once in love in his youth,' gave 'definitely "queer" parties' and 'had a large share of femininity.' Sattherwaite is killed off in 1936 in *Cards on the Table*, thus meeting the fate of almost all homosexual characters of his era.

Of course 'queer' carried more mixed connotations in Christie's time than it does today, and there is a strange lack of specificity to some of her sexual references. In the eponymous novel in which Lord Edgware is disposed of, the word 'queer' is used frequently and Lord E. has a butler 'who might have posed to a sculptor for Hermes or Apollo' and reads the works of Casanova, de Sade and a book on mediaeval torture. It is unclear whether Christie is hinting at homosexuality or rather a generalised middle class fear of unspecified sexual depravity among the upper classes.

The queerness of Agatha lies in the way in which she suggests another and less ordered world lying beneath conventional middle class English prejudices and class structures. Poirot's obsession with order—he once remarked he would prefer eggs to be square than round—resonates with the theory that detective fiction is about restoring harmony. But like Miss Marple, who constantly reminds us that evil is everywhere and can discern a mass murderer through his resemblance to the newsboy who teased cats in St Mary Mead, he also knows that civilisation is a thin veneer that at any time can be threatened by human greed and irrationality. Both of them would have made superb analysts. As Christie wrote in the preface to *Cards on the Table*, one of her favorites: 'The deduction must, therefore, be entirely *psychological*, but it is nonetheless interesting for that, because when all is said and done it is the *mind* of the murderer that is of supreme interest.

When I am falling ill one of the early signs is a desire to reread Agatha: even if I remember who did it, there is still pleasure in watching how cunningly she leads us to the eventual denouement. I shall deeply miss being able to share rehashing the fine points of her plots with Dorothy Porter.

Rigozzi

On How Original Sin Made the West

An excerpt.

JAMES BOYCE

The idea that there is something wrong with us, not because of what we do but who we are, became one of the more surprising pillars of the secular world.

ILLUSTRATION *by*
LEIGH RIGOZZI

created live at the Book of Days workstation

ON HOW ORIGINAL SIN MADE THE WEST
3.30 – 4.10PM, FRI. 22 MAY
CURIOSITY STAGE, PIER 2/3
HICKSON RD, WALSH BAY

Also appeared at:
— *THE BODY: SIN, SEX, DENIAL*
— *THE EVOLUTION OF BELIEF*

JAMES BOYCE is the author of *Born Bad: Original Sin and the Making of the Western World*. He is the multi award-winning writer of the bestsellers *1835: The Founding of Melbourne and the Conquest of Australia* and *Van Diemen's Land: A History*. He has a PhD from the University of Tasmania, where he is an honorary research associate of the School of Geography and Environmental Studies.

THE WESTERN WORLD is the first culture in human history to forget its own creation story. I say this even though I am fully aware that you, like virtually everyone else in Australia, has heard of Adam and Eve. Indeed they are, with their dangerous apple and sexy fig leaves, two of the select group of Biblical characters, up there with Noah and his Arc and Jonah and his whale, to live on in popular culture.

This is true, but my point is that there are many understandings of Adam and Eve. They are the central characters in a number of *different* creation stories. Muslims, Jews and Eastern or Orthodox Christians share the account recorded in Genesis but not the Western world's interpretation of it. It is this understanding, different not in the outline of events, but in the essential message and moral purpose it takes from these, which is now largely unknown. Indeed most Western people do not even know that we have our own distinctive tale of the beginning of humanity, let alone know that this account was the foundation pillar of an equally distinctive spirituality. Even committed Christians and knowledgeable historians prefer to see Western religious inheritance through the prism of the so-called 'Judeo-Christian heritage', a concept so broad to be near meaningless.

We are not talking today about the truth of evolution. Lets take the science on that as settled. What we are discussing is the power of creation myth and how this shapes people's core sense of who they are.

If you are unclear about this just pretend for a moment that we are talking about an indigenous culture. Some of you might actually be Aboriginal, and others will come from a non-Western background, but this exercise is still relevant as it seems these days as if everyone is expected to become at least part-Western, for better and for worse. I suggest this strategy of temporary detachment from being a Western person because sensitive intelligent Australians, the sort of folk who come to writers festivals, are actually pretty good these days at understanding creation stories as a genre. We are slowly, very slowly, learning to live with the dream time. At the very least most of us now realise that Aboriginal creation stories are essential to how Aboriginal people understand their place in the universe, their relationship with the natural world, each other and themselves. And we can accept this, while NOT expecting modern Aborigines to believe that the dreamtime stories are literally true or in full agreement with contemporary notions of morality. We accept that Aboriginal people can uphold modern science and morality, but still affirm the importance of their creation stories. We accept that these stories concern a different level of meaning, which is so ingrained in the culture, that it is simply not possible to simply *reject* it and move on, even if this was considered a desirable objective. Rational argument about the truth or the morality of the story, or even actual knowledge of the story, might be important in certain contexts, but in the sense I am talking of today, it is beside the point. Indigenous people are not autonomous, come from nowhere, clean slate beings. Indigenous people have a cultural inheritance, grounded in their creation myths, which shape consciousness itself. And so, I dare to suggest, do we.

TO START we need to go back in time. Back to the dying days of the Western or Latin speaking part of the Roman Empire. Those heady days of the barbarian invasions when the secure imperial universe, which had seemed like it would last forever, was coming to a close.

You will probably know that the century before this occurred the Emperor Constantine had converted to Christianity and in the decades which followed, with many ups and downs, the Catholic Church became the dominant religion. However it is important to realise two things. First, the Catholic Church did not have a monopoly of religious belief even in the West, there were still plenty of pagans and competing Christian traditions. And second, even within the Catholic Church there were many traditions and not yet one clear set of consistent teaching or dogma, even about the most fundamental questions of all—What was the meaning of Christ's life, death and resurrection? And what did it mean to be saved?

While there was much diversity and overlap, two broad streams of spirituality can be identified, each of which had their own creation myth underpinning them.

The first stream began with Genesis 1: 'So God created man in his own image, in the image of God he created him; male and female he created them'. In this tradition, which became the dominant stream in eastern or Orthodox Christianity, the emphasis was on the essential goodness of creation, including human beings. Sin disguised and distorted this goodness, but it did not change its essence. Salvation was about uncovering or seeing the truth, recognising and knowing the divine spark within all of life. In this tradition, a new born baby revealed the face of God.

The second stream began with Genesis 2, a second creation story with a different history which is awkwardly placed next to Genesis 1 in the Bible even though it contradicts it. Here man is created first, then woman from his rib. And then in Genesis 3 we have the famous Fall, when, you know the story, the serpent tempts Eve to eat the fruit from the tree of good and evil and she, because she desired 'to gain wisdom' and know good and evil, ate the fruit from this tree and encouraged Adam to do likewise. Adam and Eve then became conscious moral beings, ashamed of their nakedness, and were banished from Eden.

If you haven't looked at this story for a long time I urge you to read the text again, as literally as you possibly can. It most obviously seems to be a story of the human journey into consciousness, from a position where we are not burdened with morality, into a state where we are. Eve does not seem the baddie at all, but the representative founding hero of humanity, risking all for wisdom despite the risk of death and the disapproval of her creator. Adam is the follower, following in the steps of his gutsy partner. And for many people over the centuries, the story has in fact been read like that, or more straightforwardly, simply as a warning about the serious consequences of disobeying God.

If you do reread these passages (easy to find since they are right at the start!) you will also discover, perhaps to your surprise, that the word sin is not used even once. The interpretation of the story which we have absorbed, that Adam and Eve sinned, and that because of this they and their descendants, including us, became sinners, is not an obvious reading of the text. When we remember the story we reveal the influence of a residual cultural memory of the western interpretation of the story.

I tell this journey into dogma in *Born Bad*, and we don't have time to go into it here. But to understand the creation story that shaped us, and still shapes us, it is important that you know that it was only in the early fifth century that Augustine's teaching about the meaning of the Fall, and how we needed to be saved from this, what was called the doctrine of original sin, became Catholic doctrine.

The doctrine of original sin taught that Adam's sin (taken for granted misogyny required that Eve be given a subsidiary role) was passed onto every human being and that because of this inherited sin, God was as angry with us as he had been with Adam. No matter how good we tried to be, no matter how outwardly moral our conduct, divine wrath could not be avenged. Sin infected every good action, every noble deed, every attempt at abstinence, because we were sinners through and through, and justly on our way to eternal hell.

So what was the face a newborn baby in this tradition? The face of a sinner.

Now the point of this teaching was not to show how innately bad for its own sake. The point of the creation tale was to show why we ALL needed salvation in Christ. When you think about it, it is actually not so easy explaining why

Christ died for everyone. What about good and decent people? Why did they need Christ too, or more specifically, baptism in the Catholic Church. Surely God could not be angry with holy people? Original sin overcame this dilemma which had troubled theologians for centuries. We all needed to be saved because we were all sinners. It was not just that everyone sinned, but that everyone was a sinner.

Here could also be seen a belated and long sought for justification for the already widespread popular but unbiblical practise of infant baptism. Why did babies incapable of committing a moral act, need to be washed clean by Christ?. Finally there was an answer.

Moreover, this answer conveniently ensured that, as the sole representative of Christ on earth, only a Catholic Church baptism could guarantee salvation. Be you pagan, barbarian or dissenter, better to be safe than eternally sorry. What sort of parent would not take this precaution for their child? And once baptised, like it or not, you were a member of the Catholic Church for life. And in these uncertain times, when secular sources of authority were collapsing, there was also some earthly solace and protection in this.

I hope I have made the essence of the doctrine of original sin clear. It is an upside down difficult to comprehend moral code. It is the only religious teaching that I know of which divorces actions and choices from morality. You are in essence bad not because of what you do but who you are.

"Silky's got some
Pop Biscuits – and
I've made some Google Buns.

How Enid Blyton Changed My Life

An excerpt.

ROBERT DESSAIX

—

Robert Dessaix talks about the enduring effect of Enid Blyton's stories on his imaginative life.

—

ON HOW ENID BLYTON CHANGED MY LIFE
11:00 – 11:40 AM, Sat. May 23
Curiosity Stage, Pier 2/3
Hickson Rd, Walsh Bay

Also appeared at:
— *ROBERT DESSAIX: WHAT DAYS ARE FOR*

ROBERT DESSAIX is a writer, translator, broadcaster and occasional essayist. From 1985 to 1995, after teaching Russian language and literature at university for many years, he presented the weekly Books and Writing program on ABC Radio National. His best-known books, all translated into several European languages, are *A Mother's Disgrace*, *Night Letters*, *Corfu*, *(And So Forth)*, *Twilight of Love* and *Arabesques*. His most recent book is *What Days Are For*. Robert lives in Hobart, Tasmania.

ILLUSTRATION *by*
ZOË SADOKIERSKI

created live at the Book of Days workstation

with thanks to Rene Cloke, whose illustrations I borrowed to make this collage

YOU WOULDN'T HAVE LIKED ME, ENID, I can quite see that, not really, but it doesn't matter—I probably wouldn't have much liked you—you were unbelievably bossy, if truth be told, beastly to your mother, your husband, your own children, and almost never left Buckinghamshire (except to play golf in Dorset)—yet, in a way, you (of all people) made me who I am. Odd, isn't it.

Marilynne Robinson—the one-of-a-kind American writer, Marilynne Robinson, says that, although she comes from Idaho, it's Cicero she's most indebted to (not counting Jesus, of course)—and you might expect me if you asked me to tell you who fashioned me (if you're familiar with any of my books at all, and coming as I do from my own private Idaho) to say Turgenev or Tolstoy (not to mention Gogol—now there was a magician), but I can't help suspecting that it was in fact first and foremost Enid Blyton. The others—along with Shakespeare—were a kind of kind of background radiance.

For meaning I've looked to others, the Galilean among them, as Marilynne Robinson did, and if you smile today at anything I say, you'll be smiling at traces of Gogol in me ... but nobody—I'm convinced—had a deeper effect on my imaginative life than Enid Blyton, whose prose was so bloodless you can just gulp it down like warm water, barely noticing what you're imbibing. There was Heinrich Harrer when I was about ten (*Seven Years in Tibet* changed me for life, certainly), and there was André Gide when I was sixteen or seventeen (*The Immoralist*, once read, can never been forgotten), and Tolstoy soon after, but first there was Enid.

Like any civilised child's in the 1940s, my life with books began with Enid Blyton's Magic Faraway Tree books—well, with *Tootle*, actually, the Little Golden Book by Gertrude Crampton about the young locomotive that is cajoled into giving up chasing butterflies and smelling flowers in meadows beside the tracks and admonished to 'stay on the rails no matter what'. What's 'chasing butterflies and smelling flowers' an allegory for, I wonder? What's 'staying on the rails' a metaphor for? Surely not ... it couldn't be ... or is it? *Well, I'm still chasing the butterflies, Gertrude, still smelling the flowers, if you know what I mean. Get the picture? Tootle-schmootle! Stand clear!*

Enid Blyton ... What was it about Enid Blyton? It wasn't the Toffee Shocks or raspberry jam, it wasn't the leprechauns or lemonade, it wasn't the gnomes or pixies—in fact, I never much cared for pixies—no, no, it was something more profound—several things, actually: yes, she knew the secret places children like to escape to, but there was more to it than that—a lot more.

Rigozzi

On Non-Monogamy

An excerpt.

LEE KOFMAN

An argument that ethically practiced non-monogamy can create relationships that are just as sound as monogamous ones.

ON NON-MONOGAMY
4:30–5:10 PM , FRI. 22 MAY
PIER 2/3 CURIOSITY STAGE
HICKSON RD, WALSH BAY

Also appeared at:
— *WRITING WHAT MAKES YOU BLUSH: WORKSHOP*
— *THE DANGEROUS BRIDE*
— *THE CRAFT OF DIALOGUE*
— *QUICKIES AND CORSETS: THERE'S MORE TO THE STORY OF WOMEN AND SEX*

LEE KOFMAN is an author of four books, including the memoir *The Dangerous Bride* (2014, MUP) about non-monogamy. Her short works have been widely published in Australia, UK, Scotland, Israel, Canada and US, including in *Best Australian Stories*, *Best Australian Essays*, *Griffith Review*, *Meanjin* and more. Lee has been mentoring writers for over ten years. She is the blogger-in-residence for Writers Victoria and her personal blog was a finalist for Best Australian Blogs 2014.

ILLUSTRATION *by*
LEIGH RIGOZZI

created live at the Book of Days workstation

THE NIGHT BEFORE my traditional-white-Jewish-wedding I went to a fetish club and kissed a girl dressed in a nurse's uniform. She was a willowy, pretty redhead with serpentine lips, her plastic uniform dangerously short. The kiss felt bubbly like champagne. We kissed among fake velvet couches and rusty mirrors. The DJ served us to the thump of *Relax, don't do it*. Our teeth clashed and the girl quickly pointed out this was my fault. I apologised, embarrassed, and tightened my grip around her slender back, sinking my tongue once again into her liquid otherness.

Kissing her was more awkward than pleasurable, but it was the awkwardness that I sought that night, the discomfort. Comfort I already had in my husband's-to-be arms. I was in lust with the foreignness of the girl. I flirted with her and also with myself, falling in lust with the woman I became when I kissed her—strange to myself, unknown to her.

And some days after my second wedding anniversary, while I was staying at a writers' residency in the mountainous outskirts of Perth, I took a male lover, embarking on a longer, more complicated affair. Still, I didn't think of myself as an adulteress, but as a non-monogamist.

I ONLY EVER WRITE books to answer questions urgent to me. *The Dangerous Bride* was rooted in my quest to find how to be non-monogamous in an ethical way, particularly given that before my marriage I'd had another, quite disastrous, non-monogamous relationship. At the time my affair with the man from Perth began, I started writing my story while also looking to interview others who had tried non-monogamy, to find how their relationships worked and what price there was to pay.

To avoid stigma, people practice non-monogamy mostly in secret; it wasn't easy finding interviewees. Still, some wanted to talk and I spent several years learning about non-monogamy, although none of my new knowledge ultimately helped me. Not long after I began the book my marriage disintegrated. In retrospect, I understand that that, and my preceding, relationship were doomed anyhow. But not because we attempted to be non-monogamous. Rather, those relationships ended for reasons of incompatibility. If anything, it was the lure of sexual freedom these two men offered me, each in his own way, that prolonged my stay with them. I explore all this in my memoir of non-monogamy, which is really a book about love.

So yes, contrary to common perceptions, non-monogamous relationships don't necessarily end for reasons to do with (in)fidelity, or don't necessarily end, full stop. Existing research, including one study spanning twenty years, shows these kinds of relationships survive at similar rates to monogamous unions. Moreover, another longitudinal study done in America, which has been going for more than a decade, showed that children too can do well in non-monogamous families, as long as their homes are stable and loving. These children are often actually likely to thrive, since in some non-monogamous configurations, such as polyamory, they have more caregivers to spend quality time with and expose them to various interests.

I am not surprised by the research findings I have just discussed. To my mind, it is naïve to think of monogamy as the only workable relationship option in a society, where we may spend so many years with our spouses, and where temptations are as rife as divorce. In these circumstances, it makes sense that some permissiveness in relationships can actually invigorate and preserve, rather than destroy, them. Some prominent cultural commentators agree with this. American author Susan Squire, for example, argues in her book about the history of marriage, *I don't*, that a lasting, supportive union might be more valuable than a faithful one. Squire asks, quite reasonably, I think:

> *Why does society consider it more moral for you to break up a marriage, go through a divorce, disrupt your children's lives maybe forever, just to be able to fuck someone with whom the fucking is going to get just as boring as it was with the first person before long?*

British literary editor Diana Athill, who worked with the likes of Phillip Roth and Norman Mailer, expresses a similar attitude in her memoir *Somewhere Towards the End*, although in a more understated tone fitting of her Englishness and her ninety-one years of age. She suggests we should broaden the concept of fidelity beyond the sexual meaning:

> *Where spouses are concerned, it seems to me that kindness and consideration should be the key words … and sexual infidelity does not necessarily wipe them out. Fidelity in the sense of keeping one's word I respect, but I think it tiresome that it is tied so tightly in people's minds to the idea of sex … There are some things, sexual infidelities among them, that do no harm if they remain unknown—or, for that matter, are known and accepted …*

So how do you 'do' non-monogamy? This question is of course impossible to answer in such a short lecture; I had to write an entire book to explore it. But here are some basic things I'd love to share today. Firstly, non-monogamy can come in many shapes—practised jointly or separately, in group sex or intimate affairs, with concurrent committed relationships or occasional brief affairs, prompted by voyeuristic sexuality or romantic longing. The list is long and curious. Following my research and my own experience, my impression now is that what matters is not the shape non-monogamous relationships assume, but to what extent couples feel secure with each other.

Still, the security factor alone doesn't suffice. There has to be some fit, or at least a sound compromise, between the expectations of spouses. It also helps if both can tolerate ambiguity, navigate grey areas and be open to ongoing change. The happiest stories I heard came from couples who cultivated their intimate space above all else, making each other feel special and their partner's first priority—no matter what. It wasn't that these couples didn't experience pain. In all stories I heard joy and heartache entwined. But then, what love isn't complicated? I came to think that both non-monogamous and monogamous happiness are possible but both are hard to come by. Yet happiness within non-monogamy might feel even more exhilarating because, as one interviewee suggested, once you break the rules in love, you're more likely to live more adventurously in other areas too.

'Teeth and things' flower-fold book
by **ZOË SADOKIERSKI**

While illustrating an essay about teeth, written by Tom Lee, I started noticing other things that look like teeth: mushrooms, corn kernels, root vegetables, rocks, etc. I began collaging these images together because it amused me. At the same time, I was teaching my publication design students how to make a 'flower fold' book. It occured to me the folds open like mouths. As you can see from the images here, by placing the sequence of teeth-collages inside a mouthy book, I'm using the book form to tell a story that you read with your hands as well as your eyes. Once you've read (or looked at) all the pages, a visual story is revealed that is greater than the sum of its parts. You can look at photographs of this book, but it's not the same as experiencing it in your hands – there's no sense of how small it is, and you lose the experience of each page gaping open to reveal a new collection of toothy-looking things.

Reading with Our Hands

An excerpt.

ZOË SADOKIERSKI

Reading a book is a tactile experience. We handle books as objects, with our hands as well as our eyes.

ON READING WITH OUR HANDS
12:00 – 12:40PM, FRI. 22 MAY
CURIOSITY STAGE, PIER 2/3,
HICKSON RD, WALSH BAY

Also appeared at:
— *THE ARCHITECTS OF READING*
— *THE BOOK OF DAYS*
— *THE AUSTRALIAN BOOK DESIGN AWARDS*

ZOË SADOKIERSKI is an award-winning book designer and writer with a particular interest in the evolution of books in the digital age. As well as lecturing at the UTS School of Design, she is vice president of the Australian Book Designers Association and writes a column on book culture and reading for *The Conversation*.

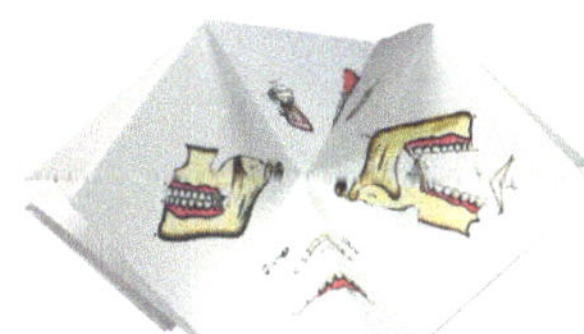

I'M GOING TO BEGIN by talking about an orange I bought in Japan. The orange was on display, protected by a fine mesh wrapper. At the counter an immaculately groomed sales assistant wrapped layers of translucent rice paper around the mesh, then carefully placed the well-swaddled orange in a little box. The box was an extraordinary piece of paper engineering, folding into itself so it closed without need for string or tape.

THE MARGINALIA ON THESE PAGES IS FROM ASTRID LORANGE *AND* MONICA MONIN'S 'LIVING INDEX'. *SEE PAGE 134*

12:01:06

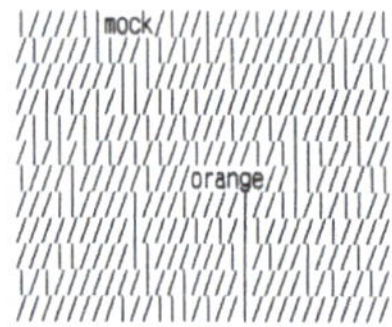

The thing about an orange is that it doesn't need packaging. Oranges are a perfectly contained fruit and their natural wrapping looks and smells appealing. But that Japanese orange was an event. Opening the box and unwrapping the delicate, uniquely textured layers felt like Christmas. It built a sense of anticipation. I became part of a ceremony—the Japanese are masters of turning simple events like making a cup of tea or giving someone a piece of fruit into a sensual, tactile experience.

The effect of that ceremony was that I considered the orange in a new way. At the supermarket I often chuck a couple of oranges into a plastic bag that take ten frustrating minutes of rubbing between my fingers to open. This experience does not afford me time to reflect on the beauty of a single orange.

If the orange is a perfect fruit, the codex book is a perfect reading technology. By codex, I mean a block of pages, bound along one edge, protected by a cover. A book, as we know it. It's light, portable, doesn't require electricity or software updates, and it's simple to use—you turn the pages to reveal the story.

A publisher once teased me, knowing I'm a book designer, by saying: *we could cover a good book in brown paper and it would still sell*. He meant a good book doesn't need fancy packaging—it's already a simply perfect thing.

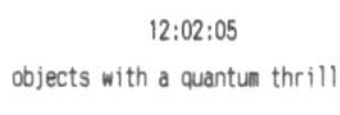

It's true. Ebooks prove this.

When we purchase a book on an electronic device, what we're actually buying is a piece of code: a digital file. That file will be loaded onto whatever device we choose to read it on: iPad, Kindle, desktop computer. It has no tangible form until it appears on our screen.

With e-publishing book design becomes largely irrelevant. There is still design involved in the process. Someone designed the template that your ebook flows into and chose the typefaces for you to choose from. Yet individual books are just floating code, waiting for a container. There is little to no unique design in an ebook. The teasing publisher was correct, a good book will sell even if packed in the digital equivalent of brown paper: a generic template.

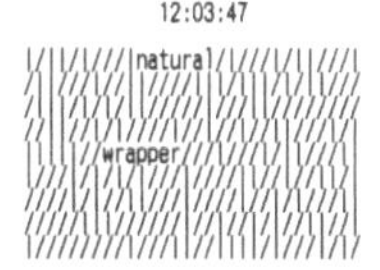

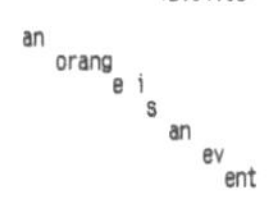

What we're talking about here is how design, or the look of a book, effects sales. Publishing is of course a commercial enterprise. The conversations I hear most about the future of book publishing focus on sales statistics: how print books are doing against ebooks, how the indies are doing against the Big Five, etc. Yet to understand the future for printed books we have to ask a different question: how do we get people to *keep reading books*? This is where design may play an important role.

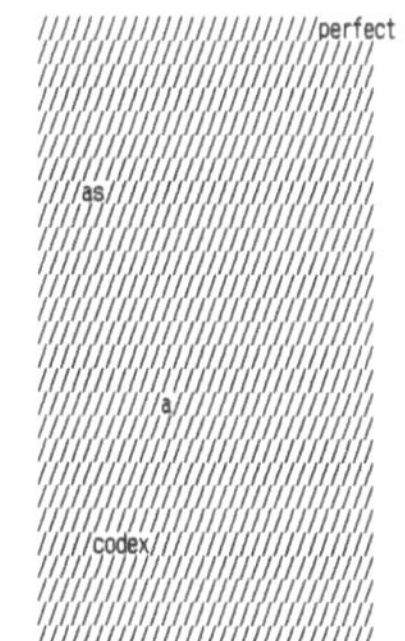

There will be no future market for printed books if people lose interest in reading on the page. My mobile phone is a portal to more reading material than I could possibly read in a lifetime. In ten lifetimes. I have a list of television series I'm

12:05:07

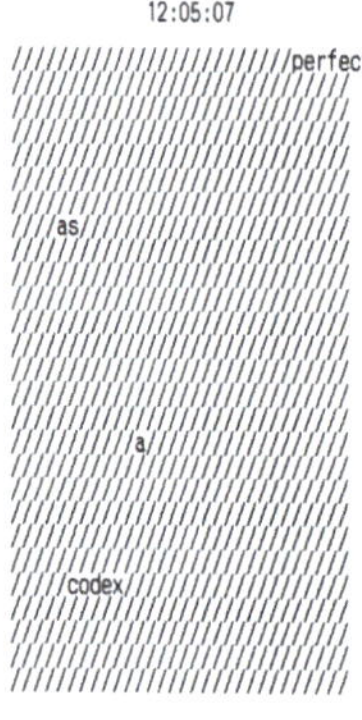

12:14:12

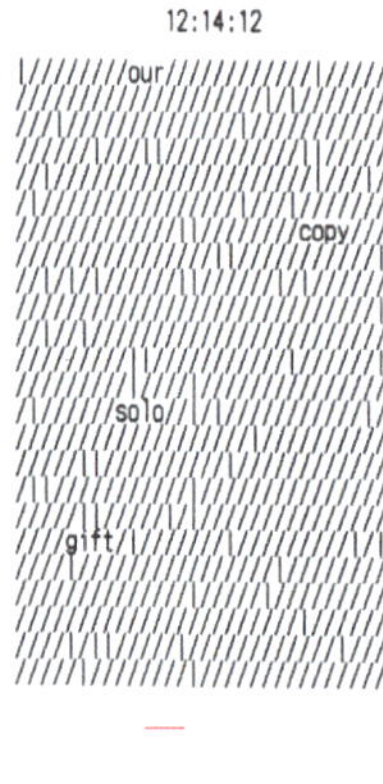

12:19:17

12:13:41

paper shuff
thumb space
no-knit telos

desperate to watch. Social media is generating gross amount of reading material every nanosecond.

To keep people interested in reading *books*, we need to foster a sense of ceremony around books and around reading. We need to make books and reading books special enough that they have a future.

Back to my ceremonial orange.

One of the things lost with e-books is a sense of *specialness*. With an eReader I'm not carrying around one orange, I've got the whole tray. If I'm online I have access to the whole orchid.

I have a terrible habit of finding great sounding articles and rather than thinking 'this looks good, I'll read it' I think 'this looks good, I'll email it to myself for some future less-busy moment' even though I know there is no future less-busy moment because I already have hundreds of things saved to read. There will never be a less-busy moment again.

The reason for this is on electronic devices, I can never do one thing at a time. My devices constantly tell me how much there is to do, demand that I keep up and interact. I don't have time for ceremony or ritual. Holding an eReader I can feel the weight of all the other books the thing contains, or could contain, waiting for me. Suddenly nothing seems special, or everything seems special.

The orange doesn't need extra packaging—the world's resources don't need the extra packaging—but the packaging creates a sense of ritual, an experience that delights my senses and puts me in a certain kind of mood: I'm focused and receptive to appreciating the one thing in front of me.

A thoughtfully designed book does the same thing. It captures me, in a focused, embodied way. These are the things I love about the materiality of a printed book. I approach it from a distance—it doesn't appear in front of me. I have time to size it up, get a sense of it in the world. I bond with it: run my hand across the embossed title of the cover, rub creamy paper stock between my index finger and thumb, feel its weight in my hands. I open it and shuffle my thumbs around until my hands settle comfortably with it. I love the singleness of purpose. There's a clear beginning, middle and end. The book doesn't network to distractions. A book exists to tell me a story. Just one story. Of course I can interpret that story many different ways, in different moods or at different points in my life I may return to that one story and find it entirely new, but the words—and images—on the page remain unchanged. There is comfort in this. Knowing that when I return to this object it will be exactly as it was.

I'm not arguing that all books should be printed—I think some books are better as inexpensive ephemeral files that can be read with abandon, then abandoned.

But in the conversation about the future of books and publishing, if we only look at sales figures, we risk placing too much attention on production and distribution profit margins and not enough on the experience of reading. A future for books is determined by a ceremonial celebration of reading, and ceremony requires objects we can cradle in our hands.

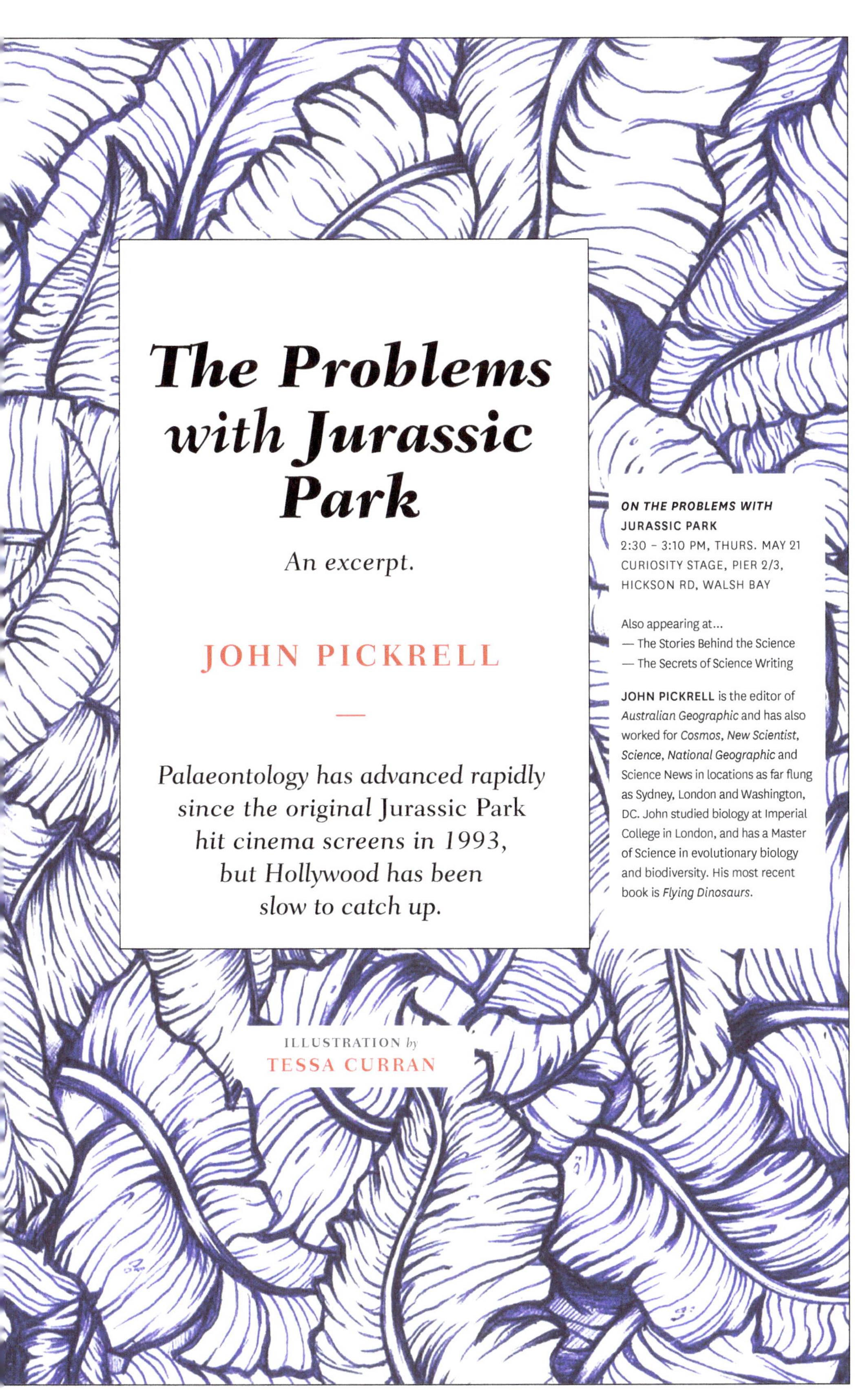

The Problems with Jurassic Park

An excerpt.

JOHN PICKRELL

Palaeontology has advanced rapidly since the original Jurassic Park hit cinema screens in 1993, but Hollywood has been slow to catch up.

***ON THE PROBLEMS WITH* JURASSIC PARK**
2:30 – 3:10 PM, THURS. MAY 21
CURIOSITY STAGE, PIER 2/3,
HICKSON RD, WALSH BAY

Also appearing at...
— The Stories Behind the Science
— The Secrets of Science Writing

JOHN PICKRELL is the editor of *Australian Geographic* and has also worked for *Cosmos*, *New Scientist*, *Science*, *National Geographic* and Science News in locations as far flung as Sydney, London and Washington, DC. John studied biology at Imperial College in London, and has a Master of Science in evolutionary biology and biodiversity. His most recent book is *Flying Dinosaurs*.

ILLUSTRATION *by*
TESSA CURRAN

Jurassic World—the fourth installation in the *Jurassic Park* film series—hits cinemas in a matter of weeks, on 11 June. It is likely to be a huge hit, but Hollywood has ignored scientific discoveries that show many dinosaurs had feathers.

In recent months, a series of trailers have been released to a dedicated fan base hungry for any snippets of information about what will be one of the massive blockbuster action movies of this year. These clips have totted up tens of millions of hits on YouTube. And the scenes that unfold in the trailers certainly promise a sci-fi adventure with all of the thrills and gory spills of the 1993 original.

Plot leaks had already revealed that the movie is set 22 years after the original film, in a fully functioning theme park filled with 'real' dinosaur species. In addition, the major predator this time,

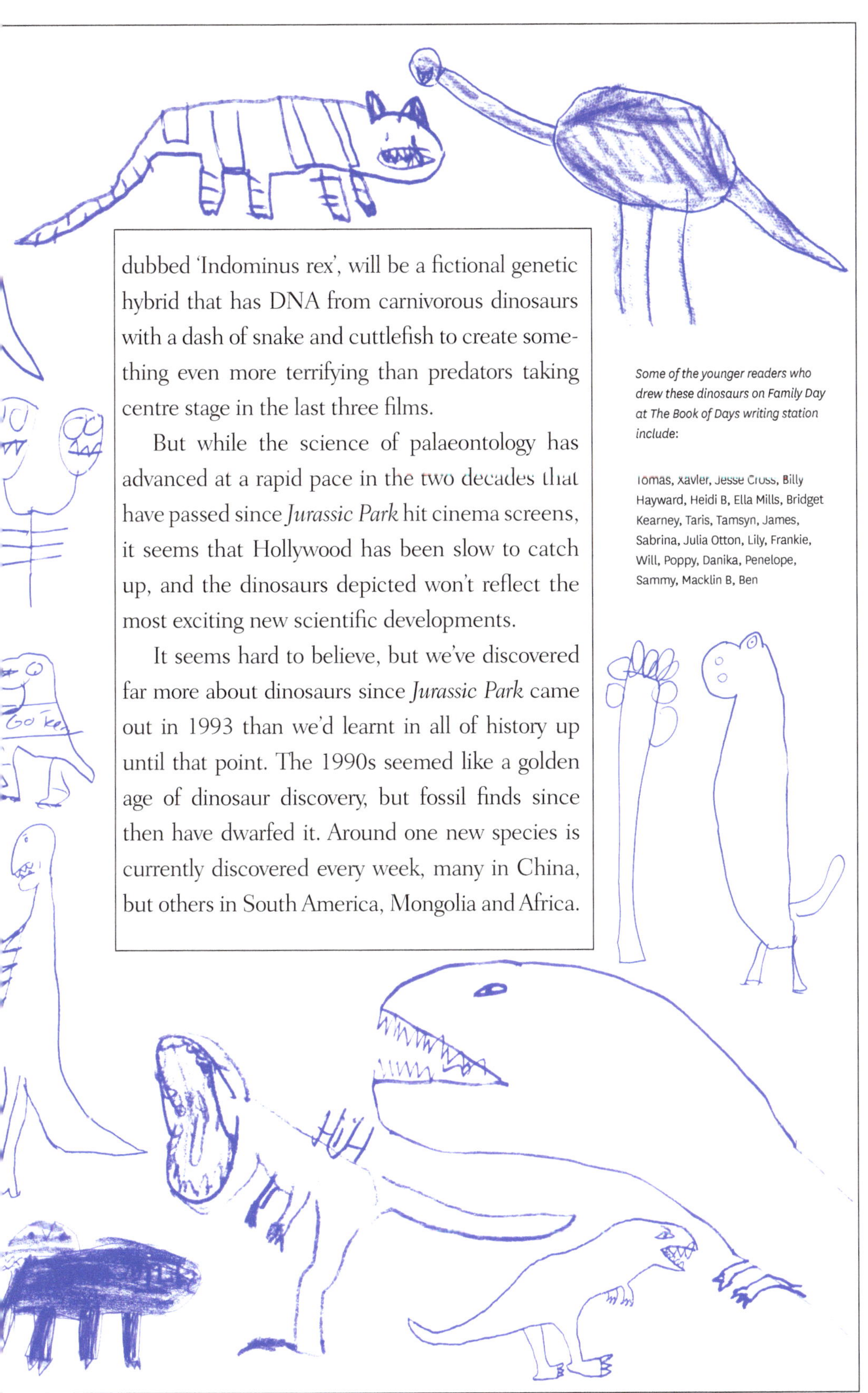

dubbed 'Indominus rex', will be a fictional genetic hybrid that has DNA from carnivorous dinosaurs with a dash of snake and cuttlefish to create something even more terrifying than predators taking centre stage in the last three films.

But while the science of palaeontology has advanced at a rapid pace in the two decades that have passed since *Jurassic Park* hit cinema screens, it seems that Hollywood has been slow to catch up, and the dinosaurs depicted won't reflect the most exciting new scientific developments.

It seems hard to believe, but we've discovered far more about dinosaurs since *Jurassic Park* came out in 1993 than we'd learnt in all of history up until that point. The 1990s seemed like a golden age of dinosaur discovery, but fossil finds since then have dwarfed it. Around one new species is currently discovered every week, many in China, but others in South America, Mongolia and Africa.

Some of the younger readers who drew these dinosaurs on Family Day at The Book of Days writing station include:

Tomas, Xavier, Jesse Cross, Billy Hayward, Heidi B, Ella Mills, Bridget Kearney, Taris, Tamsyn, James, Sabrina, Julia Otton, Lily, Frankie, Will, Poppy, Danika, Penelope, Sammy, Macklin B, Ben

Partly this reflects the fact that these parts of the world had not been thoroughly explored for fossils before the last few decades.

In the early 1990s most experts already agreed that birds were descended from dinosaurs, but it was the 1996 discovery of a beautifully feathered little Chinese dinosaur called *Sinosauropteryx* that really clinched it.

This fossil sent shockwaves around the world and left little room for doubt that birds were really just a small, specialised, flight-capable form of theropod (carnivorous) dinosaur. The finding also suggested that many dinosaurs had been feathered creatures that were much more bird-like than we had been led to imagine them. Indeed, in the years since then, more than 40 species of feathered dinosaurs have been discovered (many in China, but others in Europe and North America), revealing to us that most carnivorous dinosaurs would have

been feathered, even the *Velociraptor* and *T. rex* depicted in the original *Jurassic Park*.

We know now that not only would *Velociraptor* have had plumage, but that it would have been decked out with fans of large feathers on its forearms, something akin to small wings. Fossils revealed in 2007 showed deep pits in the arm bones, similar to those by which the ligaments of large flight feathers attach in birds such as pigeons today. While no fossils of *T. rex* have been found with feathers, we know that many related tyrannosaurs, such as a 9m-long Chinese species called *Yutyrannus*, were covered in downy feathers, suggesting *T. rex* may well have been feathered itself.

Therefore it is not unreasonable to expect that a major Hollywood blockbuster, one that had expert palaeontological advisors, might have taken some of the latest science into account. But it

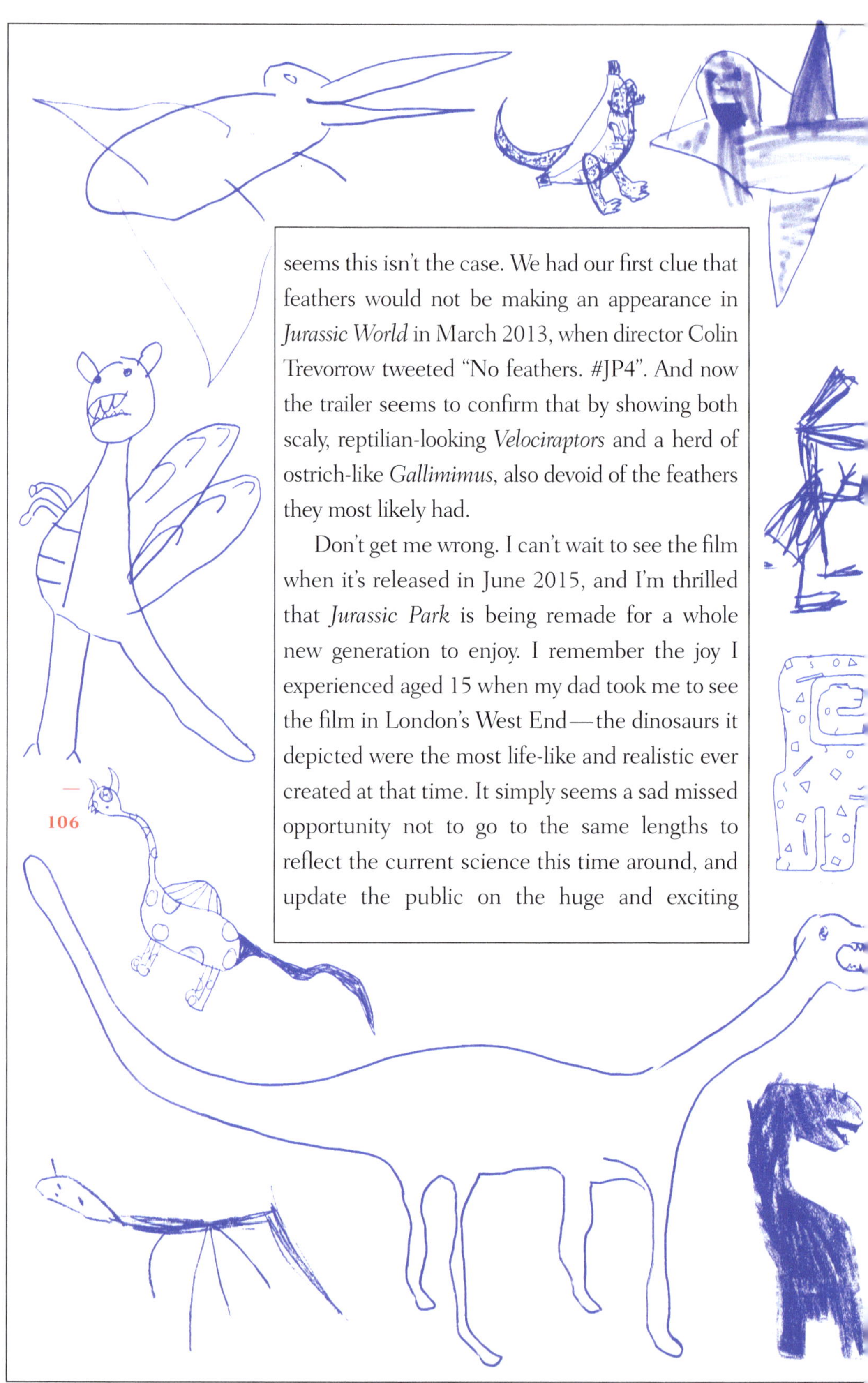

seems this isn't the case. We had our first clue that feathers would not be making an appearance in *Jurassic World* in March 2013, when director Colin Trevorrow tweeted "No feathers. #JP4". And now the trailer seems to confirm that by showing both scaly, reptilian-looking *Velociraptors* and a herd of ostrich-like *Gallimimus*, also devoid of the feathers they most likely had.

Don't get me wrong. I can't wait to see the film when it's released in June 2015, and I'm thrilled that *Jurassic Park* is being remade for a whole new generation to enjoy. I remember the joy I experienced aged 15 when my dad took me to see the film in London's West End—the dinosaurs it depicted were the most life-like and realistic ever created at that time. It simply seems a sad missed opportunity not to go to the same lengths to reflect the current science this time around, and update the public on the huge and exciting

advances in palaeontology.

There's also a wider issue here in that many moviegoers get their knowledge of dinosaurs from these films. Not to show dinosaurs as we now know them to have appeared is tantamount to spreading misinformation; and through toys, other merchandise and spin off series (and no doubt *Jurassic World* sequels) it will have a cultural trickle effect that will last for many years.

Perhaps the greatest crime, though, is denying people an incredible truth about the world around them—the fact that dinosaurs didn't go extinct when an asteroid hit the planet 66 million years ago. That there are more than 10,000 living species of avian dinosaur and perhaps 400 billion individuals flitting about on the planet right now. You only need to step outside and look up into the skies to find them.

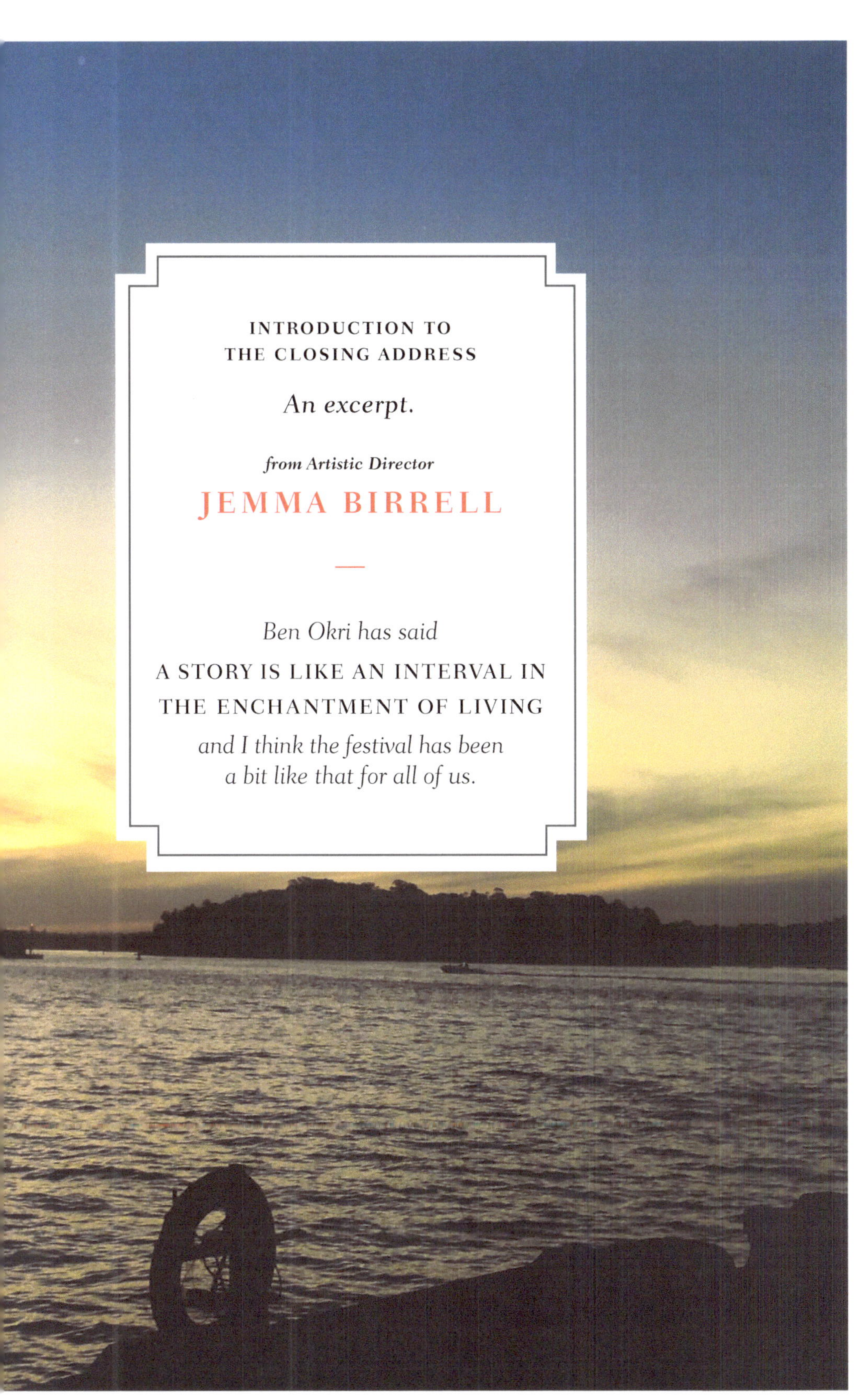

INTRODUCTION TO
THE CLOSING ADDRESS

An excerpt.

from Artistic Director

JEMMA BIRRELL

Ben Okri has said

A STORY IS LIKE AN INTERVAL IN
THE ENCHANTMENT OF LIVING

*and I think the festival has been
a bit like that for all of us.*

OVER THE PAST week there's been so many unforgettable moments: Helen Garner and Richard Flanagan getting standing ovations; audiences transfixed by Mohsin Hamid's address on life in the time of permawar; Helen Macdonald's luminous closing on nature's role in teaching us how to live; Robert Dessaix on all things Enid Blyton in the Curiosity Lecture Series; Alan Cumming getting the whole Opera House to sing *It's Saturday Night on Broadway*; Omar Musa with his stunning prose poem and Richard Tognetti playing the exquisite del Gesù violin; Ali Cobby Eckerman moving people to tears in *Give Me Back My Mother's Heart*; Anthony Horowitz giving a world first reading of his new James Bond novel; Ben Okri charming the entire theatre with his tales of magic and myth; the brilliant evening of feminist mischief and the night of the nerds; the conversations at the hotel bar and the many antics at the Late Night Salon. Then there was Andy Griffiths who was so very generous signing books for seven hours for hundreds of adoring fans. And I don't think I've ever seen so many children eager to ask a question, stampeding to get to the mics at David Walliams's events.

It was incredibly heartening to see all ages high on writing and ideas. Throughout the festival I was touched by the appreciation and warmth of readers for the writers. There was a lot of laughter and debate, and it was pretty awe-inspiring to see so many people from around Australia coming out to appreciate these extraordinary writers.

The festival has also been a time for people to catch up and for writers to meet each other, to start conversations in an event and perhaps continue them in a bar—and who knows what personal and professional ramifications these connections might have.

—

I was thrilled to present Helen Macdonald who gave the festival's closing address on nature's role in teaching us how to live.

Helen has worked as a professional falconer, assisted with raptor research and bred hunting falcons for Arab royalty. She's the author of three collections of poetry and a natural and cultural history called *Falcon*. Her recent book *H is for Hawk* has been described as a triumph and a 'wonderously atypical book'. It's a mix between a literary meditation on the writer T.H. White, a book about grief and goshawks, and as Helen said herself, a love song to the English countryside. It defies categorisation as the best books often do—it deals with obsession, madness, memory, myth, and history and is part memoir, part nature writing and part literary biography.

H is for Hawk has been a bestseller both in America and England, was named best book of the year by *The Guardian* and *The Economist* and went on to win, both the Samuel Johnson Award and the Costa Book of the Year Award. Helen writes like no other about bereavement and while it's incredibly heartwrenching, there's also a lightness, humour and visceral beauty to the prose. The critic from *The New York Times* called it a 'beautiful and nearly feral book […] that was so good that, at times, it hurt me to read it. It draws blood, in ways that seem curative.'

The language is luminous. Every sentence sings—she says 'Looking for goshawks is like looking for grace: it comes, but not often, and you don't get to say when or how. But you have a slightly better chance on still, clear mornings in early spring, because that's when goshawks eschew their world under the trees to court each other in the open sky'. As *NPR* said, reading this memoir is to have every cell of your body awake and alive.

CLOSING ADDRESS:

On Looking at Nature

HELEN MACDONALD

—

An exploration of nature's role in teaching us how to live.

2015 CLOSING ADDRESS
HELEN MACDONALD:
ON LOOKING AT NATURE
6:00 – 7:00PM, SUN. MAY 24
ROSLYN PACKER THEATRE
22 HICKSON RD, WALSH BAY

HELEN MACDONALD is a writer, poet, illustrator, historian and naturalist, and an affiliated research scholar at the Department of History and Philosophy of Science at the University of Cambridge where she teaches to a graduate level. She has worked as a professional falconer, assisted with raptor research and conservation projects across Eurasia, and bred hunting falcons for Arab royalty. Her memoir, *H is for Hawk*, won the Samuel Johnson Prize and the Costa Book of the Year Award.

Also appeared at:
— HELEN MACDONALD: H IS FOR HAWK
— BACK TO THE WILD

ILLUSTRATION *by*
ZOË SADOKIERSKI

HOW TO LOOK AT NATURE? Get out there. Pay attention. Believe it is yours. Because it is. No matter what historical or cultural boundaries are set up against you, those thriving, growing, flying, swimming things are yours too. And when you look at those things, it is good to think of their histories, and how they got there, and all the stories we have given them—the trick is to hold those human meanings in your head, and look past them to the animal itself. And the real magic is that sometimes the animals that you look at can do that for you. Encounters can be miracles.

Last week I walked up a grassy, sun-crisp autumn headland on the very edge of New Zealand. Welcome swallows carved complicated curlicues above my head, and far beneath, in a pocket of warm salt water, a bunch of young sea-lions porpoised and turned. My heart was in my mouth. There are some things you wait for all your life. I'd come here waiting for this. But I wasn't sure whether it would happen at all. The air was still. The sky a remote, blank blue. Out on the water was a fishing boat the size of my thumbnail, and my companions and I narrowed our eyes and we waited.

And then the wind came. The wind came suddenly, and it was a benison. It rolled in off the ocean and there, in front of us, a lump of white started to move. It raised awkward stick-like things covered in fluffy down and wobbled them. Wings that had not yet flown. It looked like a small child in a ghost outfit. It was a young albatross a hundred days old. For a hundred days it had sat there, looking out to sea. I thought of Theseus' ships, of the black sails coming home, and of Coleridge's albatross, and Baudelaire's albatross, and old Imperial visions of global exploration, and Romantic notions of solitude, and caught up with Coleridge's Albatross was a biting sense of human guilt at what we are doing to the natural world—for when big things happen, old stories are conjured along with the new. And the wind continued to blow and then the albatross came. The albatross came and it was too big to understand, as if a dog was hanging there in the air. It came in on the wind, long, knife-like wings bowed and webbed feet spread as rudders. It was the most astonishing thing. And as it curved in, it turned its head and looked at me with those mild, Madonna-esque eyes, down its long squid-cutting beak, and I was absolutely lost for words. Its world was wind and sea and spray and salt and the uplift from rolling swell over the southern oceans and it looked right through all the stories I'd ever been told about the world and the air shivered with its newness.

YAN QIN WENG
'ICELAND', 2012

PART TWO

SELECTED CONTRIBUTIONS *from the* FESTIVAL AUDIENCE

PHOTO CREDITS:
Jackson Mann (above) | *Chris Caines* (below)

AN **ILLUSTRATED ANTHOLOGY**
FROM THE **2015 SWF**

CONTRIBUTE BY RESPONDING
TO THE THEME **HOW TO LIVE?**
VIA TWITTER **#SWFBOD** *OR*
AT THIS **WRITING STATION**

SELECTED CONTRIBUTIONS WILL BE
INCLUDED IN THE PRINTED BOOK
AVAILABLE FROM JUNE 1ST:
WWW.BOOKWORKPRESS.COM

ABOVE AND OPPOSITE: *Posters inviting festival audiences to contribute*

FROM THE NOTECARDS

Enjoy it whilst you can. Joseph Davey, 11 years. • Don't die. • Never trust a man with two first names. • To know how to love is to know how to live. Ah yes … Pania Jeffery. It seems that the only way to truly live is to love. To love freely and widely and with abandon. In this way we make ourselves happy and we make others happy. Kerry Littrich. • With hope, love, joy, a creative play follow your dreams this was worth heading to I came from Adelaide for this! Joy! Sandy. • To be able to raise one's self above the mindless mediocrity of most people who complain, to see the beauty in each day to honour it with each breath. To be with integrity and thus respect self, the world and her many inhabitants. To know there is more than the human existence, not need proof, just trust. To observe mindfulness in your day, ensure it contains much laughter, love and magica moments. MW 2015. • Today is all you really have … now. Always do one nice thing each day (help someone pat a dog). Cherish the wonder of life. • I think the best kind of life is the sort shared with words, chocolate anc a cup of tea. • You can never watch too much tv. Jessica. • How to live? Breathe in, breathe out. • Eat less fat walk, mind your manners, go meatless 1-2 times a week. • I must create a system or be enslaved by anothe man's. William Blake. • Love your family. • Nothing is forever but life is the longest thing we'll ever experience so the secret is to just live. • By your won rules, not by ones written on white cards. • I am trying to understanc my life and life itself more generally through death. I am fearful of my own death/dying hence it feels like i infects my life/living. I am looking at the living here, all suffused with curiosity and desire. I see them as corpses too, decaying into the earth. This is a comfort as if I have the courage to look death in the eye. • Occupy space and time until you are dead, but hopefully with enjoyment. #cosmic cat. • Watch Arrested Development a lot and think every book you read is about the same things (but maybe its just you). • A moment, a love, a kiss, and also a cry. Our rights, but don't you forget … or Wrongs. TM Also, kill a snake with your bare hands and drain its power. • Live like you'd hope to live in 100 years if you held on to your age today. • Learn to respect our environment – don't be a tosser, recycle our water, better transport, hug a tree. • Always be kind and generous to those around you. By Penelope and Vicky. • How to live? With an empty mind, a smile and a kitten by your side. • With great integrity, because you need to live with yourself. • Live life to the max and enjoy it, eat well, have fun and hang out with your besties! Remember that your family loves you and they always will! Amber, age 11. • Spotted an ice-cream van, purchased a choc-nut cone, sat on the harbour front, the setting sun didn't have time to melt it, before it was gone. • You live by following these simple rules. Eat, sleep, drink, repeat. Aidan was here. • Live in freedom and peace and understand others. #sufbod. • Take care of your body, it's the only place you will ever live. • Love xxxxxxxx Miller, age 4. • You breathe, feel, taste, smell, hear, see move and either be sad, happy, angry, relieved or scared. You must have a balanced diet so you should eat junk food and 50% healthy food. Leela, age 8. • Humans are special and unique regardless of colour, religion, gender, ability or anything really. We should all live by celebrating that and what binds us, not what separates us. • be a good friend, work hard, exersize, don't get mad and help out. sharing is caring. • Smile and laugh often, love those close to and those who aren't. Appreciate beauty, wherever you find it. • drink water • Life is about you deciding what you do, what you will grow up to be and practically everything you do, chores, diet, exercise, creativity, etc. Isaac Grace. • People should live happily Freya 7 :) • To live you need: food, water, love, friends. • breathe, breathe, breathe. • Liav is not hou you have itsteckraid but I can liv with it (life is not how you expected, but I can live with it).

Ella Lucette, age 7. • In a constant state of disappointment. • In fear of ducks. • Keep calm and read Andy Griffiths. • Keep calm and keep calm. • This is a great question when you live privileged to be residing in a middle class suburb of Sydney. Attending a talk by an Iraqi refugee surgeon, Munjed Al Muderis, I realized there is one thing I can do to make a real difference in a political environment so anti-refugee and that is to teach English to these stateless people so they can have a voice in their own destiny and not remain the voiceless victims of heartless politicians. • Live so that you may bring some light and if possible, meaning to others' lives as well as your own. It is always important to look back at events in your life and realise that what's done is gone forever so regrets for what has been missed are pointless. Celebrate the past but use the present and the future to make lives better. John Nance • Live as if you only had a month left on planet earth, as if your beloved, dream of dreams was at your side, as if your heart way fully open to love and being in the now, reconciling yourself with friend and foe, replete with gratitude and giving your shadow side its due. Gus Roule. • With zest and authenticity. Nadja Temperance Jones. • Every day it rains with every food you want, you can never get too fat and then the next day you see the water filled with chocolate sauce YOU HAVE TO LIVE LIKE THAT!!! • Never stop believing in the beautify of people, nature, and our world—but never take these things for granted. Let the sheer enormity of the Earth and all its living breathing beings humble you. Existence is a miracle. • Remember that we judge others by their actions and ourselves by our intentions. Lauren. • Get a dog. Ali. • Give less of a f—k about people/things that don't matter. Give more of a f—k about people/things that do matter. BK. • By defining the word 'success' for yourself and living by your own rules. • Give others the benefit of the doubt. Life is so full and so mysterious and so connected, that even we don't know why we do the things we do. • Claudia Howard loves book. • Marina and I were at the fortune teller. Waiting outside to see him, when she turned to me and she asked. What do you hope to learn? How to live, I said. She was silent. But clearly disappointed. • Gib jedem tag die chance, der schouste deines lebens zu werden. Mark Twain. • One round of golf and a bottle of red per day is just ideal. • Be here now! Bring you rmind to the present moment, all that really exists and inhabit it fully with every sense you possess. Kerry Littrich. • Be Happy laugh out loud (LOL) have peace be Healthy. Seyrina. • Model the behaviour and values you want to teach and instil in your children. • um, in the jungle? Elkie, 4 years. • Get out of bed each morning. Eat food (make sure it's tasty!) Talk to people. Learn stuff. Make stuff from what you learn. Get better at it. Respect each day! Adam. • The best way to live is with others. Love your family, I know I love mine! Evie. • fanging to the beach. • In tassel boots (pref. suede). So many sassy, octogenarian women here. • The aim of life is not to live forever, but to create something that will. •

FROM TWITTER

Gustave Flaubert: Be regular and orderly in your life so that you may be violent and original in your work. • Your Mum. @Ann_dLandes. • How to live? Me: Just keep moving forward, and have empathy. @scslocum. • When Churchill was asked to cut arts funding to support the war he replied 'then what are we fighting for?' • Blend fearlessness, capability and curiosity. Live and love there. @ispytreasure. • Listen to the silver-backed fish robed in jade and slipper sun beneath the grey piers of the finger wharves. Listen to them sing. @john boland. • Living shouldn't be about rules or guidelines. It is about tapping into the essence of one's soul and finding your true path. @CharT_skies • We forget to look at our own inner worlds and appreciate the mental labyrinths of everyone else's. @CharT_skies • The simple question is ...how do you want to live? @CharT_skies • Family day at #SydneyWriters Festival ... a little girl just left this thought on how to live: Paris is the life. @Zoe_Sadokierski. • Nabokov: After a good deal of writing or reading I often enjoy a continuous series of extraordinary bright fluidly changing pictures. • Chuck close: inspiration is for amaters, the rest of us just show and and get to work. For Tim, Andy + crew. @Zoe_Sadokierski. • Live with Gusto. Especially if Gusto is an attractive Italian who knows how to cook. @ NickyArnall. • Brett Whiteley: Life is brief. By my god thursday afternoon seems incredibly long. • How to live? On the line: printing signage for #SydneyWriters Festival 2 hours before it starts. @Zoe_Sadokierski. • '...there is no big lie. There is no system. The universe is indifferent.' Don Draper. @MikeyMikeD. • In Vivo Veritas. @ jolpt. • Almost every dog ever: like someone left the gate open. @georgh. • Liz Fichera: When you can't enter through the front door, kick in a window. • Louis CK on how (not) to live: Everything's Amazing Nobody's Happy [video]. • You must be prepared to work always without applause. Hemingway

SHARE YOUR THOUGHTS ON
HOW TO LIVE

SHARE YOUR THOUGHTS ON
HOW TO LIVE

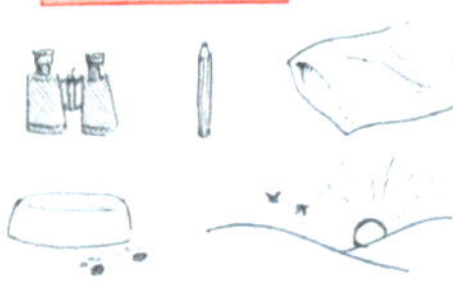

SHARE YOUR THOUGHTS ON
HOW TO LIVE

SYDNEY WRITER'S FESTIVAL PATRONS

COLOUR OF
PATRON
HAIR:

WHITE
NOT WHITE

Writer

SHARE YOUR THOUGHTS ON
HOW TO LIVE

SHARE YOUR THOUGHTS ON
HOW TO LIVE

SADOKIERSKI VS
WILSON.

SHARE YOUR THOUGHTS ON
HOW TO LIVE:

ALL METHODS LISTED BELOW HAVE BEEN TESTED BY VANESSA BERRY

*Keep alert to coincidence
*Greet cats, magpies & all creatures encountered
*Make notes
*Find out what was there before you
*Believe in luck but not at the expense of having actual plans.
*Have talismans
*Remember the names of trees
*Don't worry (too much)
*Write fan letters
* Be good to typewriters
*Follow the bus route to the end of the line at least once.

Claudia Howard loves Book.

try ry.fail. try again. failbett

try. fail. try again. fail better. - a mangled quote from sa samu el beckett

h ave lowexpectation s and you won8t be disa' disappointed'

FROM THE TYPEWRITERS:

I have no insights myself, just a head full of other, wiser people's words. And I think that's okay. • Live … that's all you can do. No one makes it out alive anyway. • After the Alan Cumming and Damian Barr talk I'm left wondering if a human heart can truly be open if it does not experience suffering. Not all who suffer can overcome the pain of their experiences or turn it towards love and forgiveness but the kindest people I know have not lived charmed lives and the same is true of those who have shared their pain through the creative arts. Why should this be so? Are there people who have never endured suffering who are capable of true altruism? • Loving the human connection. Bethan 22 • Sever toxic relationships! • I say no to shame. • Try. Fail. Try again. Fail better.—a mangled quote from Samuel Beckett. • Have low expectations and you won't be disappointed. • Be happy in your own skin, and enjoy your own company. • I spare existentialism for Sundays. It allows me to live a peaceful and naïve majority of the week. Don't trust a man with two first names. Kate Kazokas. • Act and talk in a way that your youthful self would see you as a god or goddess. Be the person your five year old self would want to be. • From the moment you are introduced to life, it is a mystery to the moment you perish. Life cannot be explained, only lived. Life meaning is not important, those who strive for meaning find themselves lost. The best artwork is a mystery. • The way to live is to hug your daughter as much as possible. • sonder (n): the realisation that each passerby has a life as vivid and complex as one's own. • Passionately, completely, with all your heart. Honestly, ethically, morally. As if you might die tomorrow. • Never grow up. • Pile up little happinesses as you go through life, instead of waiting for the big happiness to find you. • Love with the fullest, roundest heart. Fill it with all the water in all the oceans and cry it out when it breaks. Then do it all over again, because that is how to live a full, bright, bittersweet life. • You only live once but if you do it right, once is enough. • The old wear red. • There is no way to say how to live … you just have to do it and hope you leave a lasting legacy. • With an ethical enthusiasm for live and others. • Friday, torrential rain. A day for TRUE literary tragics. • The way to live is by breathing in and out. • Live thy neighbour figuratively. • By feeling your feet on the ground, the air in your lungs, and by smiling at everyone around you. Everyone is like you—happy, sad, hopeful, lost … • By being willing to slow down and willing to looking below the outer surface of people. • So nice to hear typewriter music, I love the sound. Mechanic and

Les reading with the whoosh of the trains in the background on the Bridge. • Be gentle on the earth and know your tiny place on it. Be mindful of the environment and respect its greatness. Be gentle with your language and the words you speak. Your words need not be harsh nor your message dark. Be gentle to others and their dreams, you need not obstruct people's hopes, ever. • You should be drunk or hungover or in the process of getting to one of the two at all times. • Take a moment each day to look closely at your surroundings. Can you see the bubbles of froth on your coffee or the veins on the back of that leaf? Embrace the moment. • Do not waste time on housework! • Surely for any reflective person this is a lifelong question. Perhaps the question is best when divided into sets: How to best live the life for me; How to best use my gifts and talents and make a good life; How to live the best life for me in the context of something bigger than me. And these are just a few ideas that come to me with HOW TO LIVE. One of the joys of reading and hearing writers talk about writing their writing is sharing—finding similarities—being provoked to think anew and so much more. • Just live each day more simply so that others may simply live. P Yogananda. • How does one live? At first it might seem like a simple question to ponder on. But each one of us is different. Our soul's unique paths thrusts us into different directions. But the simple answer to all this is … just enjoy life! Charlotte Tai. • By knowing that there are not limits, there is not highest or lowest, no challenge not worth undertaking, no area that cannot be brightened, no love that cannot be found. • With an open mind and heart—curious, tolerant, compassionate and good humoured. • With awesomeness! Anon. • What is life? How does one live? The simple question is … how do <u>you</u> want to live? How to you want to be remembered? How do you want to be treated? Charlotte Tai. • Remember, you are not allowed to believe in coincidence anymore • Don't live how anyone tells you to live. Revolt against the revolting. Argue against the inarguable. • Never refuse a slice of cake when offered. • Mind your manners, go meatless once a week, walk with purpose, drink water. • To feel life, more than I see of or think it. I seek others who also feel life, even if they don't know it yet. I just attended Christina Lamb's event on Afghanistan and her experience as a foreign correspondent. People want to live in peace and if they are lucky to live in peace they should be more considerate towards war zones and war stricken people. I heard someone saying Pakistan is a big threat and is more dangerous than Afghanistan. It's their opinion but it tells me how different people think, their different notions. Through swf you get to know different ideas and perhaps that can help to more understanding of how people see and interpret. With love, Senai … a Pakistani. • We should live always with one abiding thought, to not hurt others. Whether physically, emotionally, verbally or psychologically the very best way to do this is not to put yourself first, rather put yourself last. • Everything I know about life … I learned in death. • Do not spend your days dissembling in being anything other than yourself. Life is just too damn short. • To discover the variance and successes of others, experience to discover how other people live. We create empathic understanding for community well being and happiness. @bitter.sweet.alive. • Make the most of relationships – at the end of the day, its people who matter. Enjoy the outdoors—don't get trapped into living life indoors … there is so much to love—be PRESENT! How to live? With no regrets. • So my name is Irfan Yusuf. I have no idea exactly how to live on this or any other planet. I might find the answer in what I read but more than likely all I will get is the trigger to an answer. Hopefully I will live long enough to read enough to find the right trigger. Khudahafiz. • 'We read to know we are not alone' said a wonderful author. So thank you for SWF! (But hat is happening ot our municipal libraries? Leichardt has gone techno … you check out and check in your own books … no sign of human life! Pity the kids studying librarianship today … the species is (apparently) becoming extinct; going the way of leaf tea! Who has time to brew a tea or talk about books to a librarian? Jan Murray. • If the world is our oyster, what is your universe? How many oysters can be in one universe? How to live? Garden, love, eat all the delicious things, talk to all the awesome people, be interested and engaged, laugh a lot. Be the living. • 1. Naps; 2. Books; 3. Tea; 4. Small animals (inc. humans); 5. Sunsets; 6. Birds, insects, flowers and other curiosities; 7. Other small moments of delight. • life is basically a long series of mistakes, so live by making lots of mistakes. Also live by having lots of fun and loving lots of people. • With love, compassion, joy. With appreciation and an open heart and mind. With no judgement or complaints. With laughter. With friends and family to help, support you, love you in return. With a willingness to enjoy and excite yourself. With a few indulgences. Most importantly, with love and care for those you don't know as well as those you do. • Our day at the Sydney Writers Festival. What we did first; we caught the ferry here and mum says it's a lot more peaceful than yesterday when she came with Madiline because it wasn't rainy and windy when we arrived we lined up to see david walliams and get my books signed also got a photo with him and I posted it on instagram only 2 seconds later I already had one like. Whne it posted it we were having lunch we went to a place called Lotus we had the best food ever we had these really nice prawn and zucchini pot stickers yummmm!!!! Then we went and bought these doughnouts infact it was 6 for $5 but when they gave me five I was thinking either I'm really cute or she can't count any way we started to walk here an don the way we looked for Collin and we found him and had a chat. Then we came here and so far I have read a 125 year anniversary of national geographic then I saw this when I finished my hot chocolate about five minutes ago I saw Tony Flowers. Thank you for reading and this is how you should live!!!! By Byron Lawws. Ps. I didn't read what we were meant to write about so I just added that at the end!!!! • I live in fear. Fear of life. Fear of failing, and fear of achieving in equal measure. I long to live without fear of the consequences of my actions, as this only leads to inaction. Just like the characters in my favourite books. Bold Heroic and damn the consequences. But I am paralized and so I can only read and dream, of the day I can escape my fear. • The first breeze of a light wind changing, now that is a soft feeling, a good feeling of omens … a milky cappuccino, soft serve on the harbour front, to live now. • The way to live life is without fear or fervour. To throw yourself into the abyss that is life and continue on despite all. • How to live – don't overthink things. Gather people things, and memories. Surround yourself with good people who make you want to do good things. • In a word deliberately. With the recognition that choices made will inevitably live themselves out as denials of possibilities. You have to give up on things to allow other to come into being. • You need to be comfortable with death, because that comes to us everyday in a thousand ways, plans and dreams become things missed.

Leigh Rigozzi

SOME NOTES *from the*

SYDNEY WRITERS' FESTIVAL STAFF

at the WRAP PARTY:

Don't let the muggles get you down – Ron Weasley. • We have too great veneration for cloudlessness – Ruskin. • 3 questions that should be banned from Writers' Festivals: 1. What time of day do you write? 2. What advice would you give to an aspiring writer hoping to get published? 3. Where do you get your ideas? • A comment is not a question. • SWF 2015 has cracked all box office records in the thirteen years since its incorporation. The book is certainly not dead. Or at least readers who like standing in lines to hear authors will ALWAYS be with us. • As a sound ap the SWF is the easiest gig, cause it's just mics. As a sound ap, the SWF is the hardest gig because everybody has to hear every word. I love it because it's full of ideas and there's no music. R.T. • Haven't I done enough? Tim. • H is for: Hawk, Happiness, How to live, Hell yes, Hopeless, Honey, Hokey Pokey, Hopscotch, Hairy, Horrific, Hostile, Haughty. • Things I have learnt of late: Do whatever makes you happy as long as you don't hurt anyone else; Embrace fear, but trust your instincts; You are the only person you have to live with, so like yourself and remove the toxic people in your life; Life it too short to pretend you don't want the last slice of pizza. • This year's festival taught me to worry less, appreciate slams of a different kind, reconsider the funeral industry, never trust politicians, finish more books, how to work in the arts! • Like, how do you make friends when you're a real grown up? • We don't compete with one another. There is already way too much competition in the world.

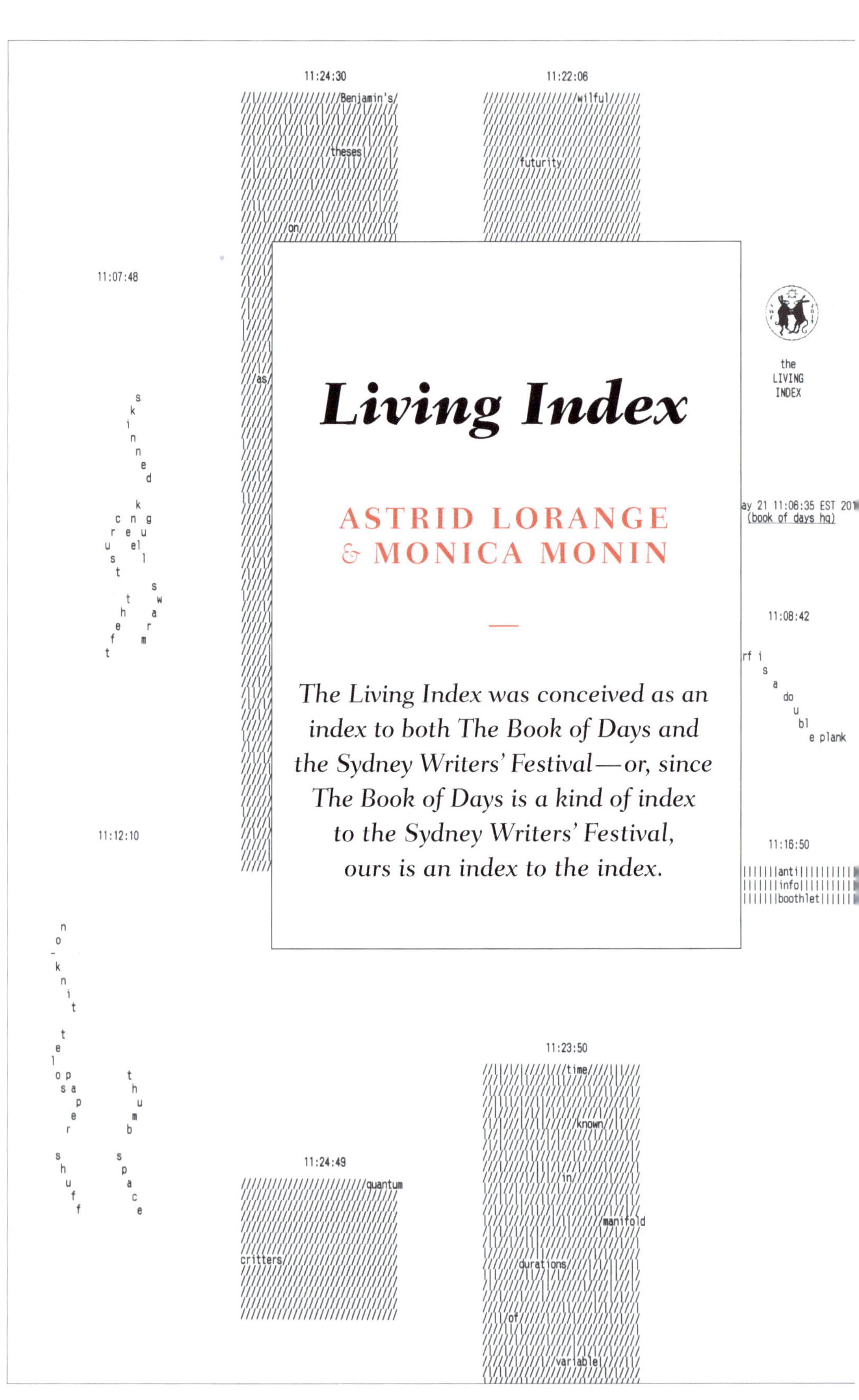
11:24:30
Benjamin's
theses
on
as
11:22:06
wilful
futurity
11:07:48
skinned
swarm
theft
the
LIVING
INDEX
Living Index
ASTRID LORANGE
& MONICA MONIN
The Living Index was conceived as an index to both The Book of Days and the Sydney Writers' Festival—or, since The Book of Days is a kind of index to the Sydney Writers' Festival, ours is an index to the index.
ay 21 11:06:35 EST 201
(book of days hq)
11:08:42
rf is a double plank
11:12:10
11:16:50
anti
info
boothlet
no-knit
thumb
space
11:23:50
time
known
in
manifold
durations
of
variable
11:24:49
quantum
critters

THE INDEX was constructed over the course of four days and in response to sessions at the festival. Astrid attended events and tweeted in response. Some tweets were direct quotes or appropriated language, some critiques of the argument being made, some responses to a trigger or concept associated with the event. The tweets took one of three predetermined text-forms: list, phrase, proposition. Lists gathered together unlike objects and subjects coalescing in the discursive space of the event; phrases reflected the aesthetic oddities of extemporaneous speech; propositions were editorial interventions into the discussion. Each text-form had a corresponding symbol (list = :, phrase = *, proposition = ~) included as the first character of the tweet to aid its later translation by a program. Additionally, each phrase was designated a number between 0 and 9 to denote relative distractedness, where 0 denotes an undistracted, directly-relevant phrasal association between the event and the tweet and 9 a totally distracted, entirely irrelevant association determined by fantasy/external influence/memory/desire and so on. Each proposition had a variable scale of tentativeness: a 0 denoted certainty and 9 uncertainty regarding the claim being made.

Each tweet, with its text-form symbol and, when relevant, its distracted/tentative variable, was translated by a program coded by Monica and then printed by a thermal mini-printer in a long continuous roll. The printer and its paper roll were installed on a long plank of wood on two trestle legs — a work station for a poem machine. Monica's

12:15:04

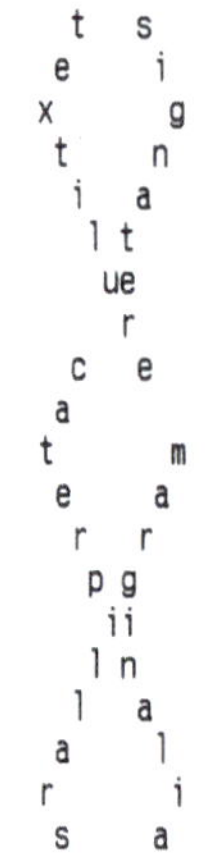

: signature marginalia, textile caterpillars
A list text-form

12:20:05

a
too
th
is a
m
orpho
logica
l ca
t
eg
ory

~4 a tooth is a morphologial category
A proposition text-from with a tentative variable of 4

12:22:30

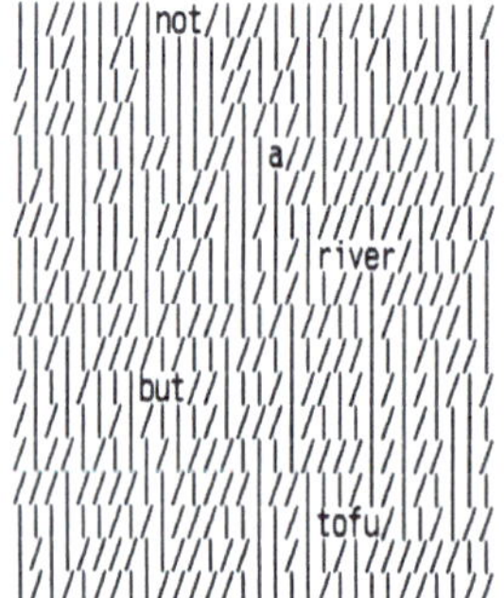

**4 not a river but tofu*
A phrase with a distracted variable of 4

code determined the formatting for each tweet. Lists were formatted in an unstructured way with their unlike items displayed as threads that wave their letters down the common space of the page. Phrases were formatted with vertical and slash symbols denoting the variable levels of distraction, producing a kind of visual rendering of the 'noise' of interference. Propositions were formatted left to right as per a printed sentence but with rising tentativeness causing a vertical drift such that a tentative proposition drops down letter-by-letter in a semi random order.

The Living Index lives in two senses: as both a real-time register of the festival and its manifold ideas and also as a system capable of transforming according to its internal demands and logic. The approach changed over the course of the four days and can be changed further by re-translating and ordering the data according to different conceits/concepts. The idea of the Living Index is to account for an experience and its archival after-image.

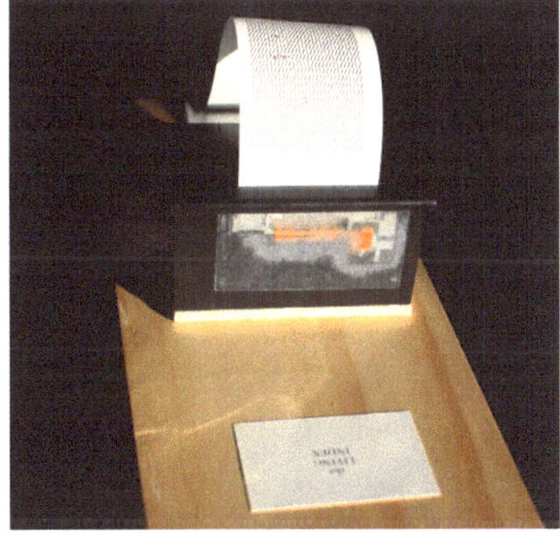

Photographs of The Living Index at the Book of Days workstation:
CHRIS CAINES

12:06:53

v
e
ry
lo
o
s
el
y
a
tr
ue
m
urd
e
r

12:08:26

living

fidelity

of

the

actual

event

11:44:45

cold

hard

fax

11:37:20

pack
of
the

11:44:13

e
m
p
a
t
h a
y r
c
o
f o
f
r
e b
a r
d o
e w
r
s
h
i
p
v
i p
r r
t o
u x
a i
l m
a
i t
n e
t s
i s l
m n o
a i m
c f m i
y f oc c
u
e sr
m hl
a oy
i u
l t q

Thu May 21 11:32:53 EST 2015

A Pack of Lies: Narration in Fiction,

Sydney Dance 2

```
////||||/crowdly/|/|/|///|/|//
/||///////||//|/|///////|||//|
////||/|//|//|||/|/|//||////||
//|///|/|////|//||||//|/|//|//
//|//////|//////|/|/////|//|/|
//|||/||///ripple///|//|//////
/|////////|/|/||/||///////|/|||
/////|////|//////|//||/|/|||//
/////||/|////|///||/|/////|////
|/||////|////|/|||/////////|||/|
//||||||//|////|/|//or/////|/|
///|///|////|/|//////|/|/|////
||/////|/|////|||/|//|////////
/|//////||/|////|///////|//|//
/|/||||||///|///||/|///|/||///|
///||////|||///|/||affect/|//|
/||////|||/||//||/|/////|////|
/////|////|/////|///|///|/|///|
/////||////|///////|////|///|/
||/|///|/|////||/////////////
//|||//|/||///||//////|//////
//|//|/|/|///|||//|vapour//|/|
//////||///////|||//||/|/|//|/
|///|//||///////////|||///|/////
//|/|//|///////////////|/|/|//
/||//|||/|/|/|//||||/////////|/
```

14:00:01

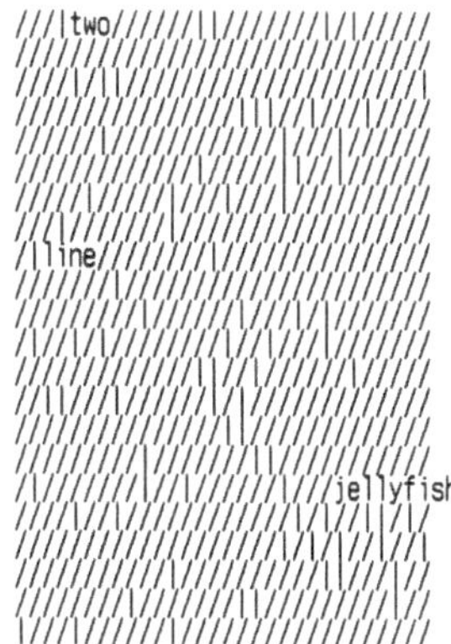

14:10:28

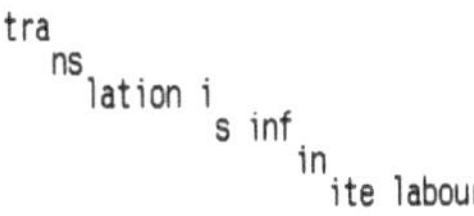

14:00:30

Fri May 22 13:27:42 EST 2015

Poetry Panel, Main Stage Pier 2/3

12:13:39

robots against class war

12:14:22

business

of

a

heart

doublet

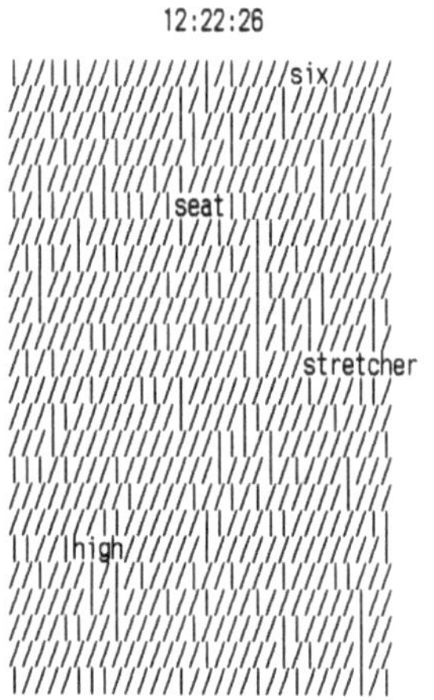

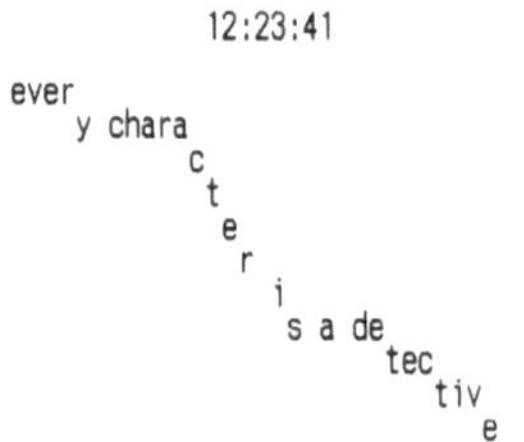

Sat May 23 12:12:29 EST 2015

Australian Story, Club Stage Pier 2/3

13:52:24

a dad is a wormhole

13:36:32

13:38:30

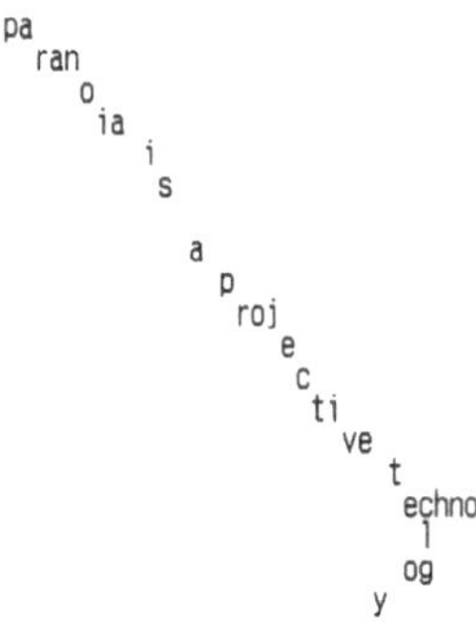

14:03:37

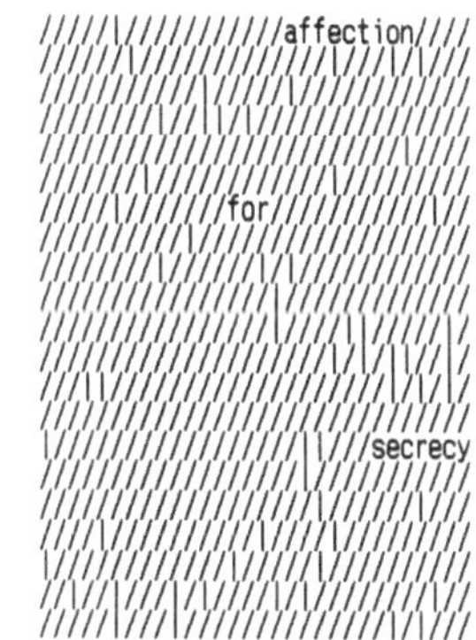

13:53:21

no high sc
hool for
small capital
ist
s

Sat May 23 13:36:04 EST 2015

Åsne Seierstad, Dissecting a Crime

Pier 2/3 Main Stage

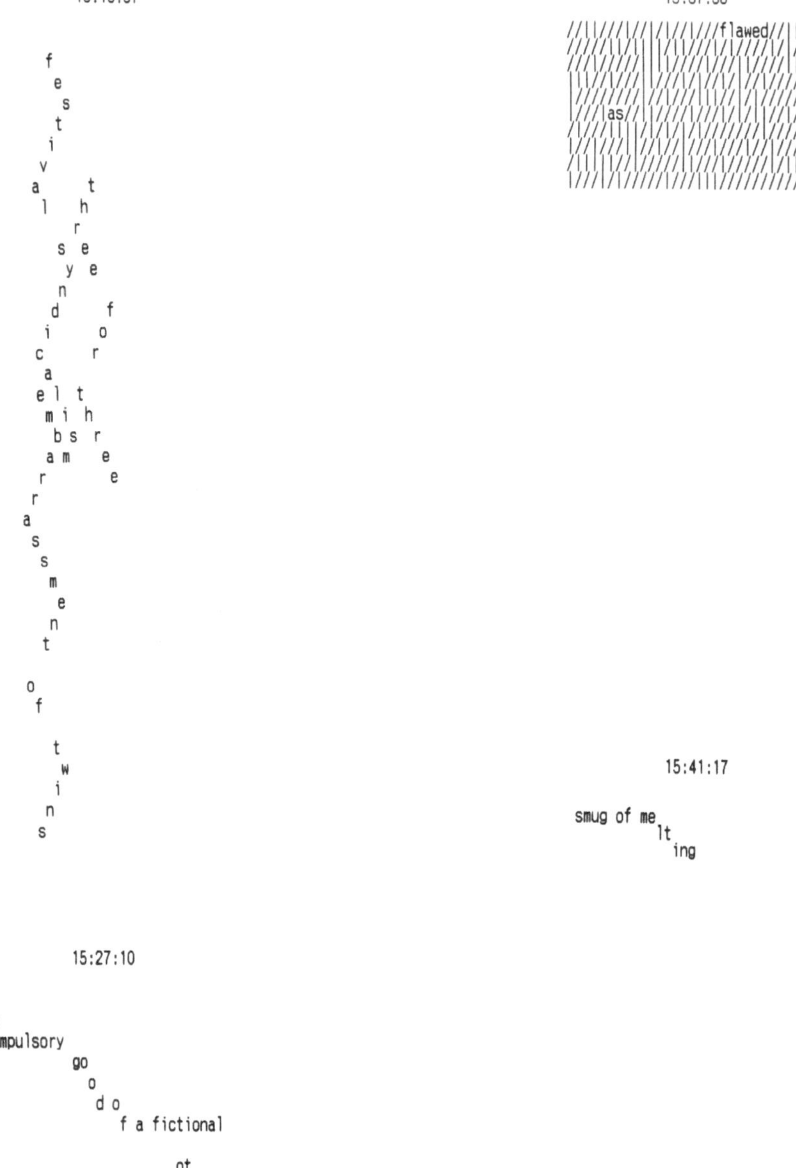

Sat May 23 15:10:44 EST 2015

Funny Girl, Sydney Dance 1

11:52:12

ra
t
he
r
80s creamy and g
ar . . . .

11:45:56

```
        1
       0     d
      0       j
l
 o     o      r
  n     d    e
 g       d  q
             u
l      r    e
i     e      s
f    c        t
e     i    f
  m  p    l
 g  a  e    a
 l   s  s  v
o   t      o
b  e      u
e  r     r

t  b      b
 e  l      o
  c  o      n
 h   g     e
```

11:38:40

aioli

as

an

index

of

deceit

12:20:29

two
hundred
year
sustainable
clam

11:46:56

a rec
ip
e is
a plot-driven
st
o
r
y

Sun May 24 11:37:16 EST 2015

Slicing and Dicing,

Main Stage Pier 2/3

www.ingramcontent.com/pod-product-compliance
Lightning Source LLC
Chambersburg PA
CBHW061032100726
47911CB00006B/159

9780994286758